In many ways I don't recognise myself from who I was in February this year. There will always be pieces of me that need working on, stuff will continue to come up, but I can make a conscious choice as to how I will react and respond.

I know I don't have to follow my negative thoughts. My day to day life is now calm and peaceful, a description I've never used before.

I've reconnected with my spiritual life and I'm reconnecting with old friends and nurturing new friendships. I'm creating boundaries for the first time. These are not inflexible but support me to live peacefully and do the things that are important to me.

Wendy

I didn't have huge difficulties in life, nor major obstacles to overcome, just a general feeling that life was short and that I wanted to make sure I was living it to the fullest. Through her work, I think I'm on the way to this.

I've learned to let go of things in the past, and concepts that I'd previously read about such as living in the moment and gratitude have become part of my makeup.

Fiona

I improved my meditation practice and I walked every day. I joined a 12-week exercise and nutrition program, continuing for a second round and lost 16 kilos over six months.

I undertook a daily gratitude practice. I turned my mindset around. All the little steps I have taken in the different elements of my life have come together and made a big impact on my life.

Keeping it simple and breaking it down has meant I have been able to focus, and not feel overwhelmed by life.

Start small and just keep growing and building. Every bit counts.

Michelle

Meditation was introduced to me by Fiona as a key centre point of a desperately needed focus on self care, for myself in all areas of my life.

I was lacking any sense of focus or purpose and I was living a life that was not paying off in so many ways. I found meditation at first embarrassingly hard and I thought that I didn't need it or that it wouldn't do much.

However, by making time to make sure I meditated regularly, helped me realize that it is vital to my self care routine and the simple act of ensuring that I make space for it has had a huge flow on effect to each day, by being able to feel more grounded.

I am able to tend to my mind, check in to how I am feeling and set my tone for the day ahead. I also meditate before I go to sleep each night which reaffirms the fact to me that I am worth caring for, which then affects other decisions that I make in regards to my health and wellbeing. I am very grateful that meditation is now a regular habit and my go to if I feel I am needing a reboot!

Kim

FIONA REDDING

the
happiness
hunter's

Guide to Meditation

*How to connect with your most powerful
resource to eliminate stress & anxiety,
while increasing energy & focus*

GRABB
PUBLISHING

Reading this book may change your life forever…

Dora Altintas

This book is dedicated to:

Ariston & Vivienne; my two little sparks of inspiration
for change, and to keep going.

My mum, Helene and dad, Michael
(I can do what I do, because of you).

Chris Raine, for HSM, and everyone at HSM
with me in the trenches through those early days.

Dora Altintas, for helping make the book a reality.

This book is also for Dr. Issam Kadamani… for everything.

Contents

The Happiness Intention

*"May this be a space for connection
to our heart; for unconditional love,
happiness, kindness, acceptance,
forgiveness, compassion and peace – for
ourselves, each other & for the world."*

About the Author: Fiona Redding

By her own admission, Fiona's journey into business has been a pretty interesting road in many ways, and there were many points in which it would have made more sense logically to just go and get a "real job".

Yet it was an unshakable faith and trust in the path which she had chosen that kept her metaphorically and literally putting one foot in front of the other.

Fiona's faith in her mission and purpose has, and continues to be rewarded; The Happiness Hunter walks (the beating heart of The Happiness Hunter), are now across Australia.

With a coaching and healing business helping other people change their lives, Fiona also runs retreats and workshops catering to clients both locally and internationally.

Her work receives regular national interest and media coverage (including television, print and podcast interviews), and Fiona facilitates practical and inspiring workshops and delivers high energy and impactful keynotes, based on her own real-life learnings and experiences.

In addition, she co-hosts #BusinessAddicts – the Podcast, with close friend and collaborator Loren Bartley (at the time of writing this book, they celebrated the publishing of their 100th episode).

However, if you ask of her greatest achievement, Fiona will quickly attribute this to the respectful and successful co-parenting of her children.

"I have an excellent relationship with my kids' dad and their stepmum; we are successfully co-parenting to raise these two amazingly kind, loving and resilient human beings. My relationship with all of my family is now built on love, acceptance, forgiveness and respect – which is not how I used to see it or feel it."

At the age of 42, Fiona is the fittest and healthiest she has ever been or felt in her life.

"I have come to a place of love and acceptance for myself and I genuinely love my life. I am grateful for everything. It is an incredibly peaceful place to be in and I know that I am here today in large part because I started meditating and committed to it."

This book and the upcoming book (The Happiness Hunter), have come to fruition from repeated requests to learn more about Fiona's journey and process of turning her life around, including the question she is most commonly asked;

"If there was one thing I could do to change my life, the one thing that would make the biggest impact. What would it be?"

Her answer is always the same – meditate.

"Meditation helps us to follow our hearts, while still using our smarts."

"That is the simple secret of happiness.

Whatever you are doing, don't let past move your mind; don't let future disturb you.

Because the past is no more, and the future is not yet.

To live in the memories, to live in the imagination, is to live in the non-existential.

And when you are living in the non-existential, you are missing that which is existential. Naturally you will be miserable, because you will miss your whole life."

Osho

My Story

January 21st, 2013.

Anybody who has read my work, worked with me or heard me speak, will know the significance of this date.

It was the day I decided to stop drinking.

You see, for me, a glass of wine had long past its' social status, and I had developed a problem with keeping it in moderation. Drinking alcohol had been a considerable part of my identity for all of my adult life, and increasingly it had become my only way of coping with what I thought my life had become.

Problem drinking does not discriminate, and it certainly did not with me.

Not by age, gender or income and certainly not by relationship or parental status, and as I have discovered over the years; I know my experience of this is not unique.

A bottle of wine a day (and counting) had become my normal and my first drink was getting earlier and earlier each day. It had always been a bit like this for me, but somehow I had been able to function at a pretty high level and achieve things in my life. But it was like the wheels were really starting to fall off, and the hangovers were getting worse and a real sense of fear and desperation was starting to pervade my life.

This was not how it was meant to be.

My children were tiny, I felt like I wasn't mothering properly. I was overweight, unfit, unhealthy, unhappy in my relationship and I had completely lost my confidence in my ability get any of it right. I struggled to get work and just couldn't see a way out of our financial situation.

This was not how I had planned or wanted to live my life, and certainly not the life I wanted for my children. The truth was, I never had a plan for my life. I had just drifted along and hoped somehow that things would pan out for me and I would be happy and successful in life.

January 21st, 2013 is the day I stopped drinking. A significant date and a pivotal moment.

*"Our days and lives are made up of
a series of moments. Each moment
presents to us a choice, of how we want
to live and experience it."*

For me, the choice was to drink or not to drink, and before this date, I said yes more than I said no.

The significance of this date, moment and decision however was not in the terms of what I stopped doing.

It was what I decided to do instead. A decision that meant that my life would and could never be the same again.

That one thing was meditation.

So while giving up drinking was a very important thing to do, it was the meditation that created the real space for me to start to change my life. It was the meditation that opened me up to begin exploring other ways of understanding myself.

The most important thing is that I became aware of my thoughts as being separate from me and I stopped believing every single thought in my head. From here, I learned that just because I have a thought, it did not mean I had to obsessively think about it, or use whatever means to deny or suppress it.

What followed was the practice of becoming aware of my thoughts, and catching them before they grew legs and went on a rampage through my mind.

"Accept – then act.
Whatever the present moment
contains, accept it as if you had chosen
it. Always work with it, not against
it. Make it your friend and ally, not
your enemy. This will miraculously
transform your whole life."

Eckhart Tolle

Not long before I started meditating, I had already made a major decision, which was to start my own business.

This came as a result of over 12 months of looking for work. Spending hours putting together applications for jobs that I never heard back from (not even in the form of a rejection letter).

"Every adversity, every failure, every
heartache carries with it the seed of an
equal or greater benefit."

Napoleon Hill

I had enough to ask myself the question – how could I think more laterally about this, which in turn resulted in the question of "how could I match my skill set to self-employment?"

Starting a business came from a place of necessity (it had never been a dream or life-long desire); I simply wanted meaningful part-time work to match my qualifications.

Yet it was this decision which provided me with a glimmer of hope for a future that I could create. One that would be far different from the barrel of the future life that I felt like I was staring down.

It provided hope that maybe other things could change too.

It was the motivation I needed to make radically different choices about how I was living my life.

"What we think, we become."

Buddha

Life Before And After

Before I get into the impact of the simple and powerful practice of meditation, there are three things I feel you need to know:

1. I was a sceptic, and the last person I would have ever bet to undertake a meditation practice.

2. At this point, all I wanted was to be happy, I wanted to be an excellent role model for my kids and I wanted to be living in a loving environment.

3. The decision to stop drinking didn't happen overnight, it had been brewing over a period of time. I knew that something seriously needed to change, but it took many months of trying to moderate and cut back before I was able to accept that the drinking thing wasn't working out for me anymore and was just creating a big mess in my head.

In my head, my life was a nightmare, and this was mirrored back to me from the external world too.

*"To many, total abstinence is easier
than perfect moderation."*

St Augustine

Deep down inside, I knew I was using an unhealthy and self-destructive habit to drown out the chaos and noise in my mind.

This space was my contrast. Contrast is powerful. Contrast is a gift.

So, if I didn't want that, what did I want instead?

While I had repeatedly heard meditation was powerful in so many ways regarding our mental, physical and emotional health, I was skeptical, but thank goodness, still wise enough to know that I needed to replace a bad habit with a healthy one.

My start into this journey was as utterly simple as it was essential. I downloaded two guided meditations, and listened to them on rotation.

I felt the shift and benefits almost immediately.

My practice has evolved over the years, with the benefits becoming more profound as I expanded my learning on this single subject. The more I learned, the more I implemented and practiced, the bigger the impact… in every area of my life.

Here is the thing… I am no different to you.

Just like you, I am a human being, who has thoughts and experiences emotion, and perhaps, just like you, I muddled my way through this life.

But I came to the conclusion that how I was operating and the way I was living my life just wasn't working, that it was time to find a better way. It was time to start taking responsibility for my life and where it was heading and to really start playing my game to the best of my ability.

I wanted to know more, I wanted to understand more, and I wanted to have a different experience for my life.

I wanted to know my potential, and to connect with the potential of who I could become in this lifetime, and what I could achieve.

To do this, I had to get out of my head and into my heart.

"The moment that judgment stops through acceptance of what is, you are free of the mind. You have made room for love, for joy, for peace."

Eckhart Tolle

It was an intuition, it was a feeling deep inside me and it wasn't going away. I knew I needed to start listening and trusting in it.

I committed to meditating everyday.

I knew drinking wasn't the problem (remember, I was using it to quieten the noise and chaos). The drinking was simply a consequence of other things.

I discovered, "the thing" which we think is "the thing", is never *the thing*. Somehow, at that time, I knew that I had to look deep within myself for what my life had become, given the circumstances I had found myself in.

It was in my head and thoughts that lurked all the chatter, chaos and problems.

Through the simple practice of meditation, I was able to connect with my heart and begin to look at things from a place of compassion.

Within myself, I began to feel calm and centered, optimistic and hopeful, even as the chaos still ravaged around me in the external world.

It was from this place that I was able to change my story and perspective. The deeper I accepted, the more I shifted my perspective, the happier my life became.

I realised that happiness is to be found in the overcoming of obstacles and challenges in our lives, not in the absence of them.

> *"The purpose of meditation is not to control your thoughts, but to stop your thoughts from controlling you."*
>
> *unknown*

Our mind and thought processes are extraordinary.

We've all heard the saying "better the devil you know, to the one you don't", a saying and phrase based around the fear of the unknown and the perceived safety of the known.

It was through this journey in which I came to understand that our emotions are our own internal guidance system.

Fear is the indicator of potential danger ahead, and we are instinctively hard wired for self-preservation.

By putting these two learnings together, I realised that my thoughts of "why I couldn't or shouldn't" were born of fear and most likely fed by irrational and unserving beliefs.

It was then that I was able to acknowledge these thoughts for what they were, (my minds way of keeping me safe), and start to focus on thoughts and ideas of 'how to' instead, knowing that I was always safe.

I am now able to feel the fear and do it anyway, because I know that the fear is not real. And I know now too that the only way through, is through.

*"Courage is a love affair
with the unknown."*

Osho

The Role Of Powerful Relationships

The biggest result of my early guided meditations was a sense of peace and calm which I could experience without alcohol.

It got me wondering, if this was my result as a complete novice and beginner – imagine what I could experience if I really threw myself into it with everything I had? I devoured anything I could read and watch about meditation. I started learning how the Universe worked, seeing that everything is governed by Universal Laws… and how I had created my own reality through my own thinking.

I had started to connect with the true power of my thoughts and beliefs and emotions and feelings and focus instead on how I could create an amazing life that I really wanted to be living, instead of the life that I had unwittingly found myself living. All this, from the readily available and free information I had found.

I was hungry to learn more and I was ready to go as deep as I could into learning about it.

It was like finding the magic lamp to a world I had never before could have even imagined existed.

That I had come to this place in such a short period of time from a place of skepticism and doubt is nothing short of miracle. Not long after I started down this new path I wrote in my journal that I wanted more. I wanted to know my potential, I wanted to know who I could become in this lifetime. Setting intentions is powerful. Getting clear on what we want, on believing we can have it and on being masterful about our thoughts and thinking opens doors and creates opportunities – it's almost like magic.

Mid 2013 I wrote in my journal – "this student is ready for the teacher to appear".

And appear he did, in the form of Dr. Issam Kadamani (MSCDM. IMM (Aust.) M. NMI (Aust.) Alumni USA, Reiki & Sekhem Master, Ajna™ Tibetan Healing Grand Master).

Whether I found him, or rather, he found me, it does not matter.

What matters is that through meditation, I had created the space for him to come into my life; I was open to the possibility that someone like him could exist.

In addition to holding Doctorates in philosophy, metaphysics and theology, Dr. Issam has earned the esteemed title of Grand Master in Ajna™ Tibetan Healing.

> A master is a person who has learned to overcome the limitations of their ego. A master is a person who has learned not to listen to their thoughts. A master is a person who has trained themselves to go beyond their mind, and to experience life outside of the prison of their ego.
>
> A Grand Master is a master of the masters, who has the wisdom, experience and expertise to teach the teachers.

With this background, Dr. Issam challenges me and he challenges my thinking, beliefs and ego in a way that no one else ever has before.

Metaphysics is about going beyond your mind.

Meditation is the tool to help us achieve it.

I had found my teacher; beyond all that I could have ever imagined.

Having taught me everything I know until now about meditation, Dr. Issam is guiding me on my path to my understanding of truth and reality. Of how to understand that I am more than my thoughts, that within me is a soul that is more real than anything that my head tells me is real.

Through his teachings, I am learning what unconditional love is and am provided with the guidance, support and the encouragement to believe that one day I will have my answer, deep in my heart, to the question I ask every day – **Who am I?**

Who am I, really? - beyond the Fiona Rachel Redding that I identify with.

"Love is patient, love is kind. It does not envy, it does not boast, it is not proud. It does not dishonor others, it is not self-seeking, it is not easily angered, it keeps no record of wrongs. Love does not delight in evil but rejoices with the truth. It always protects, always trusts, always hopes, always perseveres."

Corinthians 13:4-7

I feel extremely privileged to have Dr. Issam as my teacher. His teachings of the Universal Laws, are practical and grounded, and here he was literally in my backyard, where I could attend his weekly meditation and metaphysics class at The International College of Meditation & Healing in Northcote, Melbourne, Australia.

Dr. Issam taught me how to meditate, beyond the guided apps.

This meditation guide is a combination of his teachings and my experience.

What is reality?

"If reality is nothing but the thoughts in your head, and if the thoughts in your head are not real, then in reality there is no reality.

The only thing that is real is your own spirit, the life force within you. You are not real, because you change.

So what you think is real, is an illusion inside your head.

The only thing that is real is your soul.

Your reality is a fabrication of your mind, according to your minds perception.

Basically, if the mind can understand it, the mind can manipulate it. So therefore, what is inside your head is not real.

Your soul does not change, it does not diminish, it is real from beginning to end".

Dr. Issam Kadamani

An Introduction From
Dr. Issam Kadamani

Anyone can meditate.

It is not a secret science or a mystical process. All it takes is a little commitment and a little practice.

By practicing meditation and being completely who you are, you will become more than you are now. It is the most exciting journey there is and meditation will help you discover the inner awareness that will take you all the way you choose to go.

You were born with the capacity to use your energies in a free and flowing way so you could develop your full potential for enjoying life and making the most of it.

However, through the years you lost or blocked this primal capacity and as you did part of you gave up its harmony with the Universe and became tense.

Meditation will help you explore your tension and release it. For thousands of years, ancient cultures have meditated as a means to obtain spiritual enlightenment. Today, in the East, the practice of meditation is pursued by those seeking spiritual enlightenment and awakening.

In the West meditation is undertaken for widely different reasons, ranging from relaxation and stress management, to healing of disease and to increase creativity and become more self aware.

The essence of meditation is stillness.

Through stilling the mind one can reach an inner level of peace and calm and with regular practice the meditation student can reach a deeper awareness, leading to awakening.

Often people have felt unable to meditate due to the frustration of their mind. In Buddhist teachings the mind is often called the 'monkey mind', because of its tendency to jump from thought to thought, without the ability to settle.

The mind has also been called a 'tiger', because of the struggle one undergoes to control their thoughts and the battle with the mind to tame it.

By focusing on the breath and starting a regular meditation practice, you will be able to:

1. Recognise your reaction to stress on a mental, emotional and physical level.

2. Control your reaction to stress and therefore alleviate the symptoms.

Your success in meditation will depend on your level of understanding of yourself, your desire for lasting change and your commitment to a regular practice."

*"What counts is how you see the world,
not how the world sees you."*

Dr. Issam Kadamani

*An old Cherokee is teaching his grandson about life.
"A fight is going on inside me," he said to the boy.*

"It is a terrible fight, and it is between two wolves.

*One is evil — he is anger, envy, sorrow, regret, greed,
arrogance, self-pity, guilt, resentment, inferiority, lies,
false pride, superiority, and ego."*

*He continued, "The other is good — he is joy, peace,
love, hope, serenity, humility, kindness, benevolence,
empathy, generosity, truth, compassion, and faith.*

*The same fight is going on inside you, and inside every
other person, too."*

*The grandson thought about it for a minute
and then asked his grandfather,*

"Which wolf will win?"

The old Cherokee simply replied, "The one you feed."

How To Use This Book

AT THE TIME of turning to meditation, I was at a low point in my life; physically, mentally, emotionally and spiritually.

I was unhappy. I felt deeply disconnected.

Not only did my external world reflect this, my behaviours and actions also fulfilled my negative and ongoing internal dialogue, which in turn compounded my thoughts of victimhood and misery.

All of this, in turn, was mirrored back to me, from the world around me.

I felt completely trapped in this space.

The day I decided to stop drinking and turned to Hello Sunday Morning (HSM) to help me achieve this goal, I had just one simple desire – **to be happy**.

When I first logged into the HSM website, in the process of creating a profile, I was asked to name my avatar.

I had never had an avatar before, nor had I ever been part of an online forum, and I had never considered that I would do either of those things in my life. It was a very strange place to find myself in. So I hovered for some time over the keyboard, really asking myself what I wanted to call myself.

"What was I here for?"

I decided that I was doing this simply because I wanted to be happy. I named my avatar 'Happiness' and uploaded a picture of my children as a reminder, for who and why I was doing this.

My introduction read as follows:

"I am 37, a mum of two divine and challenging souls (in just about equal measure), have just launched my own business, am in the process of a separation which I am trying to keep amicable, ready to give up the booze and take on the world!

I am choosing a life of good health and well-being, to be an excellent role model for my kids, and to embark on a much more respectful and loving relationship with myself.

Alcohol is not invited on this next stage of my life journey."

The reason I share this introduction with you is to demonstrate the power of setting intentions.

A powerful way to live is to be intentional about how we want to live. Shifting the attention from negative to positive changes everything.

Setting this positive focus on what I wanted for my life, who I wanted to become, for what and why I was doing it, changed my attitude.

As a result, my thought process changed, which in turn changed how I felt, which then changed my behaviours and actions. In an incredibly short period of time, the world around me was changed for the better.

I came to truly understand the power of my internal world over the external world around me.

Happiness, like any thought, emotion or feeling, is merely a state of mind.

So the question I would like you to stop and ask yourself now is; ***what is the state of mind that you choose for your life?***

Be honest with yourself. How does that contrast with what the predominant thoughts and feeling you currently have about your life?

Before you read any further, please take a moment to really think about this question because it is really important;

What do you actually want for the experience of your life to be?

Where your attention goes, the energy flows. So get clear about what you want for the experience of your life to be. Really clear.

And now I would like to ask you another question:

Are you prepared to do whatever it takes for that which you desire to become your reality?

I wrote this book, to not just share with you a small part of my journey and the impact of meditation in my life, I have endeavored to provide you a guide, together with what I trust, is a compelling reason (and/or motivation), for starting your own meditation practice.

It really doesn't matter where you are now, what matters is what you do with this moment now, if you really want things to change.

Nothing changes, if nothing changes.

*"And if you do what you've always done,
you'll always get what you've always got."*

What we try to do when we want to change is that we try to change a behaviour without addressing what is going on within us that is triggering the behaviour. So the change has very little chance of being successful.

Meditation is the tool that will help to give you the space to start to create meaningful and sustainable change in your life. By helping you understand your belief systems and thought processes, in turn this will allow you to start to shape a new, more positive mindset, leading to better decision making and better behaviours and actions.

And there will be many other benefits as well that will start to occur that you will begin to notice. Benefits not necessarily expected, but always very welcome.

How to use this book:

Read the book from start to finish

Approach your reading with an open heart and mind, putting aside what you think you know, or have previously heard about this ancient practice.

Keep in mind, that we demonstrate our greatest strength when we put aside what we have come to believe. To listen and learn beyond our current knowledge.

It is in this space and from this place, in which we create life's opportunities and possibilities.

Practice patience

The pathway to mastery is a mindful effort of practice.

The principle rule of the ten-thousand hours is as follows; to become world-class in any field you need ten-thousand hours of deliberate practice.

Be patient with yourself.

A consistent and straightforward act of mindful practice will develop awareness and understanding of the strength and power that lies within you, in turn leading to broader awareness and understanding of all that is around you.

*Every master was once a student,
and every student was once a beginner.*

Where you are right now, is perfect for you and your situation. Because right now is the present moment, and it is in the present moment that all the power in the Universe exists.

Acknowledge your thoughts

Be aware and make a note of any ideas, or resistance you have as you are reading. Journaling is a great practice to complement and strengthen your journey.

In this book, I have described different ways to meditate, in addition to eight different meditation scripts.

Before you dismiss any, set yourself the goal to try each one once. Acknowledge what you liked or didn't like about each one.

Make a note of what you want more or less of in each one.

Get comfortable with being uncomfortable

The number one reason why people avoid meditation is that it brings forward the uncomfortable thoughts which they have spent their whole lifetime avoiding, and yet they never seem ever to go away.

Embrace the opportunity to bring forward these thoughts, together with the feelings and thoughts they may trigger. For it is here in which the growth and magic truly does happen.

It is from this place, in which the most prominent shifts happen. For most of my adult life, I used alcohol (and drugs) to avoid my thoughts, together with the emotions and feelings they evoked.

This strategy I had engaged to manage my stress, feelings of inadequacy, my unhappiness and all the rest of it, only led to disaster.

Not only does, "what we resist, persist"... it gets louder.

I drank to dull and avoid my emotional pain and thought process, it persisted, so I drank a little more and sooner rather than later, my pain would present itself again.

My drinking increased, until the next round of appearances.

It was clear that my strategy was not working.

The day I welcomed my thoughts and embraced whatever uncomfortable feelings they presented, was the day I was able to walk through my darkness into light, to start building strength in areas I had uncovered as weak.

It is worth repeating, embrace being uncomfortable, because this is where the real magic happens.

What to do when triggered

You are going to get triggered, this is perfectly normal. Practice letting it be without buying into it.

Get curious about what comes up, go beyond your initial thoughts and feelings…

Acknowledge the feeling and wait to see what is behind the current emotion and keep going until you uncover the learning.

Look at it objectively, become a detective; what is the lesson and learning that this emotion is trying to convey to you?

Once finished, if you are still feeling bothered about it, or you find yourself unable to let it go, grab a pen and explore some more around it, or talk constructively with a trusted friend, confidant or counsellor.

Just do it

Stop thinking about it and start doing it. This not so ancient piece of wisdom is not just for your meditation practice; this applies to everything in your life.

More importantly, be consistent and do it daily.

The most enlightened sages still practice daily. Remember, it is not called meditation perfect. It is called a meditation practice!

Have fun

Last but not least, have fun with it. Remember, there are no rules to meditation, and there is no right or wrong way to do it.

It is about being ok with the present moment, whatever this moment is presenting to you.

Most importantly, have fun.

Get curious and explore whatever may present itself, putting aside judgment, resistance and the need to argue.

Fiona

Meditation

History of Meditation

MEDITATION IS OFTEN described as a systematic way of training the mind, and its presence has been dated back to an ancient civilisation in the Indus Valley (located in what is known today as Pakistan and North West India).

This is where archaeologists discovered evidence of meditation in wall art dating from approximately 5,000 to 3,500 BCE.

Artwork images depicted people sitting on the ground, with their eyes shut, and hands resting on their crossed legs.

In other words, people sitting in meditation postures.

There are also descriptions of various meditative techniques found in Indian scriptures dating as far back as 3,000 years ago.

It truly is an ancient ritual and yet, even with the evidence of different forms of meditation practices recorded in Taoist China and Buddhist India (between 600-500 BC), the exact origins and creators of this ancient tradition, continue to be a hot topic of debate amongst the historians and practitioners alike.

Between 400-100 BCE saw the compilation of the Yoga Sutras of Patanjali (the eight limbs of yoga), and the Bhagavad Gita (the philosophy of living a spiritual life through yoga and meditation).

It was via the Silk Road, which meditation spread to other cultures, influencing religions such as Judaism.

As ancient as this practice is, the terminology used today to "meditate" was not introduced until the 12th century AD, coming from the Latin word meditatum.

Introduction into the Western Society

Meditation was introduced to Western society through the immigration of the Chinese in the 1800's (also around the same time, in which you can see Buddhist thoughts in the literary works of Ralph Waldo Emerson and Henry Thoreau).

However, it was the public praise and practices of high profile celebrities such as the Beatles, during the 1960's which heavily influenced its popularity into the mainstream.

Eastern Masters who became well known in the West, like Sri Chinmoy and Osho, also played a significant role in bringing awareness to benefits of this ancient practice.

More recently, high profile celebrities like Oprah and Deepak have shared their personal guided meditations which have helped open up this practice to wider audiences.

It is now common for many highly successful celebrities, entrepreneurs and elite athletes to share the positive impact of their meditation practice on their performance and success.

Look into any successful individual's daily habits and you will see meditation appear within their top three-to-five must do success rituals.

Our interviews on #BusinessAddicts – The Podcast, has also revealed a common theme of our guests, many of whom are experiencing the greatest balance, happiness and success overall in their lives and businesses.

They have a daily practice of meditation.

What is Meditation

"Who looks outside, dreams.
Who looks inside, awakens."

Carl Jung

To understand what meditation is, we need to first come from a place of knowing what it is not.

Meditation is not thinking about or contemplating or stopping your thoughts, nor is it day-dreaming or fantasising.

It is not a religion, and yet can, (and has) been applied to many religious foundations and principles.

The power and strength of a meditation practice is in the simplicity of its process, in the form of a specific technique with the intention of allowing your mind to have a rest (note, that I did not say "stop your thoughts").

An active meditation practice follows a specific process and order to guide you to a new state of consciousness from what you currently experience.

More importantly, it produces results which can be verified.

*"Meditation is bypassing your thoughts
to build a bridge to go beyond your
mind and the activity
of your thinking."*

Dr. Issam Kadamani

Why do we meditate?

Seeking an inner peace and harmony to achieve an external peace and harmony with our surroundings and others, may be the simplest explanation.

A state of peace creates awareness.

Awareness creates a connection between yourself and the truth within you.

When we have awareness and feel connected, we are living in the present moment.

We meditate to get oxygen to the brain; to calm ourselves and to heal our physical body.

We are living unrealistic, fast thinking lives, and in this space, we operate on shallow breathing.

Stop for a second. Take a big deep breath and feel it fill your lungs. Now hold it there before releasing it fully.

Repeat that three times.

Notice the difference? Oxygen relaxes all of our body muscles.

We need to breathe deeply to stay calm and healthy. But most of the time we are too busy and too distracted even to notice how we are breathing. Meditation gives us the space to allow ourselves to breathe deeply.

The Ten Benefits of meditation include:

1. Finding inner peace

2. Increasing self-awareness

3. Grounding yourself and being calm

4. Living in the present moment

5. Increasing consciousness

6. Connecting to your intuition, inner wisdom and inspiration

7. Making your energy more active and alive, recharging your energy, and helping you become unstoppable

8. Curing insomnia, diseases and any problems

9. Spiritual connection, connecting yourself to the life force within you

10. Creating a sense of purpose, meaning and fulfilment in your life

> *"All that you are is the result of what*
> *you have thought. It is founded on*
> *your thoughts. It is made up*
> *of your thoughts."*
>
> Swami Sivananda

Why do we struggle to create stillness in our mind?

Meditation means being still, and the mind does not like being still.

Minds wander, it's what they do.

The mind's job is to keep running, to keep our body operating and to keep us alive.

If the brain stops, our physical body will die.

We cannot stop our thoughts, and neither should this be our intention. Our job is to let the mind just be and to focus on what we are doing – which is to practice ignoring the activity of our mind.

If we don't have a conversation with our thoughts, eventually they will stop insisting on having a conversation with us.

"Meditation is a connection to your inner divine. Nurture your soul through meditation and let it blossom."

Dr. Issam Kadamani

*"I have convinced myself that
there is nothing in the world…
…no sky, no earth, no minds, no bodies.*

Does it not follow that I don't exist?

*No, surely I must exist if it's me
who is convinced of something.*

*But there is a deceiver, supremely powerful
and cunning, whose aim is to see that
I am always deceived.*

But surely I exist, if I am deceived.

*Let him deceive me all he can; he will never make it
the case that I am nothing while I think that
I am something. Thus having fully weighed
every consideration, I must finally conclude
that the statement*

*"I am; I exist" must be true whenever
I state it or mentally consider it…"*

"I think; therefore, I am…"

*Rene Descartes
Meditations on First Philosophy*

Credited with these words, French philosopher Rene Descartes called his thoughts into doubt, as his previous ideas and beliefs have been proven to deceive him.

Disproving everything that he believed in, and when there was nothing left to believe, he concluded that he is still left with himself.

For the deceiver could not deceive him of his existence, because if he could, then he just could not exist. I think; therefore, I am…

It begs these questions then;

Who am I, if I am not my thoughts?

Who am I, if I am not who my thoughts are telling me I am?

Who am I, if this is not what my thoughts are telling me I am experiencing?

It's enough to blow your mind, and yet it is something that we can all relate to.

How many thoughts have you had that you logically know to be untrue, which inevitably make no sense but which you can't help but believe, and allow to determine how you think, feel and the actions that you take, or don't take.

We all have thoughts that we believe to be true. Imagine for just a second that none of our thoughts were true.

When we genuinely believe our thoughts to be who we are; our thoughts will then determine our actions.

The problem is not that we have thoughts. It is how they serve us and what we do with them which determines if there is a problem or not.

When we can learn to be more consciously aware of our thoughts and our thinking and be more disciplined with the direction we are allowing our thoughts to take, then we can start to create a happier and more peaceful existence.

Thoughts alone are neither good nor bad. It is the meaning that we attach to them that will determine whether they serve us or hinder us.

> *"Out beyond ideas of wrongdoing*
> *and right doing there is a field.*
> *I'll meet you there. When the soul lies*
> *down in that grass, the world is too*
> *full to talk about."*
>
> *Rumi*

Our thoughts are just that - an idea or a belief that has no meaning or significance, except for the one we attach to it.

It is only when we fully grasp this, then we can start to create the right environment for the thoughts and ideas that will assist us to live our best happiest, healthiest, most fulfilling and prosperous life.

"Our past cannot be changed, and to be preoccupied with it is inefficient in time and effort.

Likewise, by fretting over the future, we only exhaust ourselves, making us less able to effectively respond when the future is actually upon us.

By worrying about a mishap that may or may not take place, we're forced to undergo the event twice — once when imagining it and once again if and when we actually experience it."

H E Davey

The goal of meditation is to help us learn to become the master of our mind, rather than letting our mind control us.

I am… the two most powerful words in the Universe.

For it is what we put after them that determines our reality, and provides a deeper insight into our unconscious thoughts and beliefs.

These two words, and what we follow them with, create a self-fulfilling prophecy.

"Your beliefs become your thoughts,
Your thoughts become your words,
Your words become your actions,
Your actions become your habits,
Your habits become your values,
Your values become your destiny."

Mahatma Gandhi

Put very simply, behind your thoughts is a program, known as your belief system. There are many inputs into this program (most of which is made up of personal past experience, including childhood experiences, cultural expectations and, or societal norms).

Until you can accept the concept that the thoughts and ideas in your head do not just arrive, that there is a program that is influencing your thoughts and how you think, until you can understand this, you will not be able to change your thoughts.

Thoughts are being delivered to you by your belief system, either consciously or unconsciously.

Your reality is determined by your thoughts.

Change the non-serving aspects of your belief system (also referred to as limiting beliefs or blocks), and you consciously direct the flow of your thoughts, which in turn directs the flow of your life. This is how you override mental and emotional blocks and tap into your intuition.

Meditation will give you the space to experience yourself without the thoughts to determine who you think you are. Giving you the space to see your thoughts as just that – a thought, an opinion, and something that you do not have to believe.

Most people avoid meditation because they fear their thoughts.

They dread and avoid looking at the person they think they are. It is easier to keep ourselves busy and on the go than it is to sit quietly with ourselves, our thoughts and beliefs, with no external distraction.

Balance is achieved when we can focus on the inner and outer world equally, and to use the internal world to influence the external one positively.

A successful meditation practice is one which recognises that our thoughts are nothing to be afraid of, they are neutral, and they are merely reflecting information being served up by the subconscious mind.

They are merely a collective series of narratives, memories and self-talk and are based on our perception, our life experiences and level of knowledge so far, up to this moment now.

Perceived stories and memories, in turn, will create a whole narrative about the present moment and future events. Setting yourself up for success in meditation is about embracing and welcoming the thoughts and understanding and recognising how you have been reacting and responding to them.

It is about changing the way you think about your thoughts.

"Thought-habits can harden into character. So watch your thoughts."

Buddha

Solving Problems With Meditation

"You don't have a problem with the problem. You have a problem with your attachment to the problem."

Dr. Issam Kadamani

To overcome the problem with our attachment to the problem, we need to narrow our thinking.

So what do we mean by that?

It means we need to focus on nothing else, except the present moment.

When we are confused, we are confused in the present moment. Therefore, we need to become aware of the present moment and what currently holds our focus and attention.

When we feel lost, we need to understand and talk about the problem we are having in the present moment, with the present moment.

Not the problem we are having with the past, or the problem we think we will have in the future.

We need to focus on the problem we are having in this present moment now.

There are symptoms and signs of chaotic and unhealthy thinking and thought processes. If you are having any of these, then it may indicate that your thoughts are out of control and until you can identify them as the cause of your issues and challenges, then the problems and difficulties you are experiencing will not go away.

Symptoms of unhealthy thought processes that are not working for you:

- Regular to chronic procrastination.

- Is there something that you wish you could do or want to do, but it keeps getting put off as a someday goal?

- Overthinking to the point of paralysis and taking no action.

- Inability to focus on a single task. Constant multi-tasking.

- An anxious feeling of overwhelm and not knowing what to do next because there is so much to do.

- Ruminating on the past.

- Restless sleep and waking up feeling tired in the morning (this is a classic case of the mind not shutting down).

- Emotional outbursts, like anger, blame and sadness.

- Seized muscles, particularly around the neck and shoulder area.

- Feeling stressed, anxious, worried and a physical sense of being tightly wound up.

A sign of healthy thoughts and thought processes are ones that drive and create positive behaviours or action towards a future goal or direction.

All thoughts can be positive, despite what might feel chaotic or painful. It is merely a case of recognising these thoughts and feelings for what they are; as a source of feedback which in turn can allow us to then take a positive course of action.

Overcoming Procrastination

Procrastination is a conflict, whereby we are in a conflict of achieving something.

So if we are living in that battle, we are not going to be calm. To overcome the friction, we need to stop and recognise that there is an obstacle that is creating this conflict.

To overcome procrastination, we need to become calm, so that we can pause and take a moment and review the situation.

To create calm, and to learn how to stay calm, we meditate.

No one can really get lost. When we calm our emotions, we can move into the conflict; we are no longer lost.

For example, in the process of writing this book, I procrastinated in the most creative of ways.

I felt stressed, fearful and my body physically reacted with very tight neck muscles and headaches.

The ability to recognise that this was created through my belief system and current thought process, meant that I was able to work back and become aware of the mental state that had led to the situation.

I was now in a position to review my belief system, change my thought process or to simply let them go.

I realised that my physical and emotional feelings were feedback that there was a personal fear, triggered by the belief of not being good enough, or deserving.

The fear that was coming up for me was that I was a fake, I was a fraud, that I wasn't qualified to be writing this book – who was I to be trying to do this?

There is a name for this, one which you may have heard of: The Imposter Syndrome.

Experiencing the imposter syndrome means that you are unable to internalise your skills, accomplishments or achievements. To feel like you don't deserve or belong to be where you are.

I attempted to suppress these thoughts of not being good enough, by ignoring them. To push on through, as opposed to acknowledging them and learning to dance with them (which is a beautiful metaphor of how to work your way through this process).

Ignoring the internal thoughts did not work, they didn't go away, and suppressing them just led to those thoughts presenting themselves in a physical sense in my body.

Reconnecting with this knowledge that my thoughts are not real, but there was a belief system that was holding me back, rather than resisting it, I just decided to accept that part of myself – in fact, I started referring to it as Dr. Fake.

In my mind, I was now able to create a new story, because I felt like I was 100% qualified in that anyway… as a result, the fear disappeared.

It meant that I could accept that aspect of me (Dr. Fake) and accept that Dr. Fake might have an opinion about things. This presented me with the choice of a conscious decision to choose how these thoughts affected me.

I was able to use this feedback as a compelling and positive reason to just keep on going.

By understanding that this fear was not real, but in acknowledging and accepting it, meant it lost all of its crippling power, mentally, emotionally and physically.

Awareness of my thoughts in the present moment, allows me to understand both my weaknesses and strengths. This in turn provides the opportunity to challenge and change internal dialogues that do not serve.

A far cry from my past practice of denying and using whatever means to avoid them.

The Role of Meditation in Mindfulness

I first learned of mindfulness, or being aware of the present moment in the present moment, from the beautiful spiritual teachings of Eckhart Tolle.

Eckhart has a term for mindfulness which deeply resonated with me – he refers to it as *Present Moment Awareness*. I prefer this phrase as opposed to the word mindful (I tend to read the word *'mindful'* in its literal form; a full mind, this being a complete contradiction of the meaning).

For me, the term; *present moment awareness*, seems so much more practical, peaceful and powerful.

Our lives are made up of a series of moments, and it is in these present moments, where life is truly lived.

The present moment is where the power of our decision lives. It is the where our heart beats, and the precise moment in which we breathe.

It is in the *present* moment that we laugh, that we experience love, joy and happiness.

It is in the present moment that we take action. The only point at which we can make any change in our lives is at the present moment.

*"You are always just one decision away
from a different life..."*

unknown

The role of meditation in mindfulness is about helping us become aware of the present moment and accepting the "is-ness" of this present moment for whatever it is.

Until we can accept things for what they are, as they are, right now, then we are not ever really living.

Until we can accept things for what they are, as they are, right now, then we are not ever able to change things.

The decision you make at the present moment is the most influential decision you can make in your life.

Eckhart Tolle has a wonderful description of how we experience life and time and how we think about it. He states that the majority of our time, we spend living horizontally on a timeline – we are either looking back or looking forward – we are never in the present moment, never in the now. He encourages us to think about time on a vertical axis, to begin living and experiencing our life vertically in the present moment, living in the now.

On the horizontal axis, we merely exist on the surface of our lives.

Mindfulness (or present moment awareness), is the popular and effective way to counteract the stress in our day to day life. It works through the process of guiding us from our future or past thinking and into the vertical presence of the current moment.

Generally speaking, when our thoughts live in the past, it is often feelings of depression (excluding medically diagnosed depression), regret and guilt experienced.

In an **unhealthy** thought process, thoughts of the past can lead to feelings of depression, and guilt which can lead to sadness and anger and blame.

Mindfulness is a tool to help us make peace with our past.

A **fear-based** thought process fixated on the future can trigger emotions and feelings of stress, overwhelm and anxiety.

Mindfulness is a tool that can make us feel aligned with our future.

Making the Past and Future work for us

You may have noticed; I highlighted the following words; **unhealthy** and **fear-based** when it came how we viewed the past and future.

I stress this point as a matter of clarification and one of too much value to not mention.

Looking back on the past or into the future is never a bad thing, it's how we do this which determines if we function and make decisions from a place of emotional blocks and challenges or energised and inspired action.

Remember, how we think, affects how we feel,
which in turn determines our decisions and actions.

Healthy reflections on past event or experiences (particularly where the outcome was not what we had hoped for or is a painful memory), is to look for the lessons and learnings.

A great way to do this is to view the event as an outsider looking in, pretend you see the whole experience on a television screen. Watching yourself from an external third parties "set of eyes" detaches you from the emotion felt during the event.

It is from the place in which you can look back on a memory and take away the lessons and learnings from that experience.

Looking to the future from a healthy perspective comes from a place of anticipation of what may occur, is expected or desired, to make decisions and take action to either guide the outcome in a different direction or to confirm it.

Even from a healthy perspective, we can at times get stuck in the past and future to the detriment of missing out on living in the present moment.

The future is a present moment that has yet to be lived.

There does not need to be any fear about the future. The more we can begin to live fully in this present moment now, the more we are going to accept any future present moments for what they have to offer us – and the more intentional we can become about what those future moments may hold.

Our mind is always changing according to the commands we give, and always listening.

Repetition is the mother of mastery. Therefore, the more we repeat something, the closer we become to being an expert.

So if our thoughts are consistently negative and living in the hurts of the past, or anxious and stressed about the future – we are going to experience more of the same.

Once we become consciously aware of our thoughts, we can program a new and positive internal dialogue. Our experience and quality of life will significantly improve.

This is how meditation helps in mindfulness because meditation creates the space for us to become aware of and accept the here and now.

Cultivating a regular and daily practice allows us to be more aware of ourselves in the present moment, to become more mindful beyond just when we are meditating, allowing us to understand that our thoughts can come and go.

This is the gift of having a consistent meditation practice.

Practicing present moment awareness (mindfulness) brings us back to living in the now.

Practising Present Moment Awareness

Read through the instructions and guide below, before taking a moment to practice being present in this very moment.

- Close your eyes and to give yourself permission to go as deeply into the vertical on this present moment as you can.

- Feel the book in your hands, the texture of the cover, the pages and its weight in your hands.

- Become aware of your physical body and the points at which it is touching the seat or the ground.

- Feel your breath entering and leaving your body.

- Slowly and gently taking in as much air as you can and until you can hold no more, hold for a count of three, releasing to a count of six.

- Feel the breath leaving your body, feel your muscles contract and release as you breathe in and out.

- As you sit there with your eyes closed, listen to the sounds around you. There is so much noise in stillness. Hear all the different sounds that fill the space outside.

- Let everything else go just for a moment and allow yourself to feel this very moment.

Remember: There is no right or wrong way to do this, it is simply an act of bringing your awareness to yourself and all that is, in in this very moment.

The Myths & Truths of Meditation

> *"The cave you fear to enter*
> *holds the treasure you seek."*
>
> *Joseph Campbell*

DESPITE ITS GROWING popularity and proven benefits for mind, body and spirit, there are a few common misconceptions about the practice of meditation which prevents many people from giving it a go.

As far as myths go, these couldn't be any further from the truth.

MYTH #01:
"I don't have enough time"

In our increasingly busy lives, running from here to there, jamming as much into our schedules as possible, and with all of the distractions now available to us, it is easy to fall into the trap of believing that we don't have enough time to just sit still for ten minutes.

Because, my goodness, there are things to be done, and I'm far too busy to stop!

We are continually pushing, striving, squeezing to get more done, and then we get to share with anyone who will hear it.

How often do you receive the response, "I'm busy" to the question of: "How are you"?

How often do you provide this as your response to this frequently asked greeting?

Until we learn to challenge that belief, then guess what, the busier you are going to start to feel. Imagine if instead of wasting all that time thinking and talking about how busy you are, you allowed yourself to stop thinking and feeling busy for a brief period.

Imagine if just for a moment, that you flipped the lid on your thinking about time. Imagine for a moment that the hours in your day were a fluid and expansive bubble to be filled with useful activity.

Living in the present moment, not stressing about the past, not anxious about the future. You experience life at a slower pace while managing to get more done because you can work smarter, not harder.

You are more efficient and productive than you have ever been.

What if I suggested that meditation was the key to unlocking that door?

Does it not make perfect sense to give this a go? Seriously, what have you got to lose? Except for living in a constant state of fight or flight, stress and anxiety?

Instead, you are working and living in the space of peace, abundance and flow.

When you are ready to be honest with yourself about the real quality of your life (the one that you are truly living as opposed to the one you are showing the world), when you are ready to ask yourself the tough questions:

- How healthy are you?

- How calm are you?

- How happy are you?

- How fulfilled are you?

- How satisfied are you with your relationships?

How much you are honestly enjoying the experience of your life.

When you are ready to explore what living an alternative life to your current experience might be and how much living the way you are currently living is costing you, both in time and health.

It no longer becomes a question of not having the time; it is as non-negotiable as brushing your teeth.

To meditate, we believe that to do it properly, we need half an hour or an hour, that we need to prepare the space, and have an expert to teach us. So we quit before we have even started, because of these artificial hurdles we put in place. Making them so insurmountable that we stop before we have given ourselves a chance to start.

Meet yourself where you are. Accept that it is going to feel awkward and unnatural at first. Accept that it is going to involve a level of trust, commitment and discipline, to allow yourself that small window of time in your day.

Permit yourself to switch off instead.

The truth is…

We are uncomfortable in the presence of our thoughts, so we like to keep ourselves as busy as we possibly can so that we don't have to look too deeply at ourselves. We will convince ourselves (and anyone else within a 10km radius) that we are way too busy to stop and listen to that nonsense.

Therefore, our whole process of avoiding our own company becomes a form of self-preservation. We avoid meditating, because there is nothing to distract us from our own thoughts.

The purpose of the exercise is to not focus on our thoughts, although when we first start, it seems like that is all we can do. Our thoughts hit us hard, and we cannot meditate, so we go continue playing out the same old (boring) game of denial until we are forced to look at this practice due to falling seriously ill with anxiety or stress.

It is no longer a case of not affording the time to meditate; ***you can't afford to <u>not</u> meditate*** if you want to live a calm, healthy, relaxed and balanced life.

MYTH #02:
"I can't stop thinking, so I can't meditate"

People will often tell me that they tried it once and it didn't work for them because they can't stop thinking and so they chose to believe that meditation is not something that they can do.

It has been said that we have an estimate of 70,000 thoughts a day.

How many of them are you even aware of?

The goal of meditation is not to stop your thoughts; its purpose is to prevent those thoughts from controlling how you feel (remember; how you feel then affects the way you think, which in turn affects your decisions).

You cannot stop your mind from thinking.

Meditation is not about stopping your thoughts.

If you had no thoughts, then you would be dead. It is as simple as that.

Meditation allows you to see and understand that you are not your thoughts.

This concept can be quite a tricky concept to get your head around at first, particularly if you have never practised viewing yourself as separate from your thoughts.

The practice is about learning to accept where you are right now, and to learn to be with yourself in this present moment, and with whatever this present moment is presenting for you, mentally, physically, emotionally and spiritually.

It is about giving yourself the time and space to become aware of your thoughts and to practice observing them without attachment.

The truth is...

Meditation is about training your mental body, and to help keep you sitting in the drivers' seat of your life experience, rather than blindly following the train of your thoughts.

It is called the monkey mind for a reason. Your mind does not want you to stop listening to it, and during your first attempts, it will do everything within its power to make it as challenging as possible.

Jumping from this thought, to that thought and back again, with no rest in between.

You will struggle to sit still. Your skin may itch; you may suddenly remember every reason in the world as to why you are unable to do this, or constructing shopping lists in your head, and rehashing a long forgotten conversation.

Definition of Meditation; If we accept that we all have thoughts, and that meditation is not about stopping them, but about becoming aware of them and learning to let them go, then anyone can meditate. Yes, even you.

If you breathe, if you think, if you are alive, then you can meditate.

MYTH #03:
The sole purpose of meditation is enlightenment

When we think about meditation, we often get a mental image of somewhere in the East; a Buddhist monk or an Indian yogi.

Perhaps we will be taken to the mountains of Tibet, Nepal, maybe a retreat in Bali.

This image of meditation as a purely spiritual practice often prevents us from starting meditation, because we just cannot relate to it.

The truth is…

The practice is for far more than spiritual enlightenment; it is a scientific and systematic way to re-train your brain.

A daily practice of this ancient art-form can rewire your brains neural pathways. It will keep you healthy, helping to prevent a wide range of diseases.

It will improve your performance in any task you undertake. The scientifically proven benefits of meditation include:

Mind & performance:

- Helping you to set and reach goals

- Enhances focus, attention and ability to work under pressure

- Reduces stress

- Improves information processing & decision making

- Fosters creativity

For your body:

- Boosts the immune system

- Reduces risk of heart disease & stroke

- Lowers blood pressure

- Decreases inflammatory disorders

- Increases your energy

- Assists with ageing better

For your emotions:

- Enhances positive moods

- Helps balance emotions

- Develops resilience & emotional intelligence

- Creates a feeling of being centered and grounded

- Feeling of connectedness with others

The benefits of even the shortest periods of meditation practices are researched continuously and reported.

There is a fascinating documentary by SBS's Catalyst program called: **Series 17 Meditation: Can it Really Change You?**

Where Dr. Graham Phillips is transformed by embarking on an eight-week meditation practice as a part of his research. I have provided the website link below and highly recommend viewing it.

http://iview.abc.net.au/programs/catalyst/SC1502H017S00

MYTH #04:
Meditation is all about chanting OM

You may have an image in your head of kaftan-wearing, incense swirling, long-haired hippies sitting around in a circle chanting OM, therefore dismissing the practice as new-age, woo-woo and fluffy nonsense.

There are as many different ways to meditate as there are people on the planet, and I have a whole chapter dedicated to a few of the different meditation techniques (which does not even scratch the surface).

Your goal is to find what works for YOU.

Yes, chanting mantras is most definitely a way to meditate, and there is a study ("Societal Violence and Collective Consciousness: Reduction of U.S. Homicide and Urban Violent Crime Rates", published 2016), to support the impact that group meditation can have on the surrounding environment, called the Maharishi Effect.

It was demonstrated to show that if 1% of a community practised Transcendental Meditation, the crime rate reduced by 16% on average.

When we view meditation as a tool, as opposed to some esoteric thing that is entirely out of our ability to understand, access or reach, we then see it for the powerful tool and resource it is.

The truth is…

If the mood, moment and spirit guide you, then you certainly can find a like-minded group to sit around in your kaftan surrounding by the wafting scent of incense, chanting OM.

You can also just sit quietly in your lounge room and focus on your breath, to achieve the right outcome for you.

It's completely up to you.

MYTH #05:
Meditation requires specific and unusual positioning

Do you know how many times I have heard "I'd love to meditate, but I cannot cross my legs" as a reason for people not meditating?

All that is required when you meditate is to sit or lie down with a straight spine to allow the energy to flow freely.

Some people prefer to sit; others prefer to lie down. It is entirely up to you.

As your practice improves and you feel a desire to go deeper into a meditation practice, by all means you might choose to focus on increasing your flexibility and attempting different positions.

Right now, all you have to do is meet yourself where you are at.

My purpose and mission for writing this guide is to help you understand that meditation does not require particular skills, flexibility or positioning.

All that is needed is for you to consciously choose to sit or lie quietly with yourself, for a period of time.

To focus on your breath, become aware of yourself in your body and to spend that time allowing your thoughts to come and go, without placing any attachment on to them.

The truth is…

You do not need specific clothing, special positioning, or the ability to stand on your head. Comfort is the key.

It comes down to what feels right for you.

Start from where you are with what you have right now. Wherever you are physically, mentally, emotionally or spiritually. Just start, be open to it, commit to a consistent and daily practice, and get excited about where this life-changing practice will take you.

Meditation Techniques

> *"He who lives in harmony with himself, lives in harmony with the universe."*
>
> *Marcus Aurelius*

Different Methods of Practice

CONFUSION AND MISINFORMATION come from the fact that not only are there are so many ways to meditate. It also comes down to what you are specifically want to gain from the process.

To go deep and detailed into each one would take more than a chapter - each modality could be a book in itself.

My intention is to provide you with an overview and introduction to the different practices, to what situation or who they may most benefit. I have included a simple "how to" for the beginner.

I ask you to keep in mind, that this list is in no way complete, and to read through each one with an open mind and heart.

You never know what magic may happen as a result.

Call it an ancient ritual or modern-day success principle, one thing remains constant; the core purpose of meditation is to create a sense of harmony, inner peace, and calm.

The perfect meditation practice is the one which works for you.

The information and introduction I have provided is informational, with the purpose of introducing you to the different methods, I highly recommend you approach each one with an attitude of curiosity and conduct further research on each one, including seeking further modalities of meditation practice.

Warning, do not practice or undertake any of the meditation exercises while driving or operating machinery.

Active vs Passive

There are essentially two different types of meditation; active and passive.

Active meditation is when you are using the mind as a mechanism to control the breath or to proactively use thoughts or imagery to keep the conscious mind busy, to distract it from its thoughts. This process stimulates alpha brain wave activity.

Guided meditations or mantra mediations are an example of active meditation where you are consciously picturing or imagining things. Counting your breath is also active meditation.

Passive meditation is any meditation that follows the breath, or the flow of your thoughts, or where you are focusing on or observing another object.

Guided Meditation

Guided meditations are the most popular form of meditation for us here in the West and as an alternative to traditional meditation techniques.

A guided meditation means that you are guided by instructions and through a process to achieve a meditative state.

Guided meditation is one of the easiest ways for you to enter into a deeply relaxing state and to experience inner stillness.

It is a great way to eliminate stress and anxiety, in addition to creating the environment within yourself to bring about positive personal change.

How does it work?

You can do a guided meditation by listening to a guided meditation recording or by attending a class with a meditation teacher. Guided meditations follow a format, where you will be asked to sit or lie comfortably. You listen as your guide leads you through a visualisation meditation.

It is in this deeply relaxed state, where your subconscious is open to positive suggestions. Therefore, it is not surprising that most guided meditations are focused on improving a specific aspect of your life. Some examples of this may be for inner calm, emotional healing, abundance, success, positive thinking, tapping into your potential, connecting with a higher power, to assist with a good night's sleep or simply to just relax and let go.

Who is it for?

Guided meditations are perfect for the beginner as they require no training and no previous knowledge of meditation. They are easy to do and can bring you to a place of stillness and calm (even if you are finding it difficult to let go of repetitive thoughts, or maybe feeling stressed).

They are also of benefit to experienced meditators. Assisting them to achieve a deeper relaxation state, and is often done with the use of guided imagery to achieve goals or improve other areas of personal development.

Breathing Meditation

Master the flow of your breath, and you uncover the secret to peace within yourself and the world around you.

Our breath, also known as the respiration process, provides every living cell in our body with its life source, so that they can produce energy, repair and function.

As we inhale and exhale, our organs expand and contract, pumping nutrient-rich fluids throughout our body, including flushing out toxins from our lymphatic system.

The physical movement of breath, particularly deep breathing, not only reduces stress and blood pressure, it strengthens abdominal and intestinal muscles, as well as providing relief to general body aches and pains.

Our breath is life.

Despite being our greatest asset (and life source!), breathing becomes a task so mundane and ordinary, that its true purpose and significance can easily be forgotten.

Most of us breathe incorrectly.

During times of stress and anxiety, our abdomen will tense and prevent our larger and primary muscles (diaphragm and stomach) from working efficiently.

The secondary muscles, which are not designed to carry the full burden of our breath, are left to do all the work.

They, in turn, become stressed.

Continued shallow breathing in this state, can lead to headaches, fatigue and chronic upper body tension.

Which in turn becomes a self-feeding cycle of shallow breathing, to physical and emotional tension.

Correcting this, is as simple as breathing.

All mediation practices include the breath in some form or other; however, you will find an abundance of information on "breathing mediation" within Buddhist documents and materials.

It is said, that as a child, Buddha discovered how to enter a profoundly deep state of mediation through the observation of his breath, and it is because of this, Buddhism openly advocates this particular method.

The Buddhist meditation technique is described as Anapanasati. Broken down, this ancient Indian word means:

- "Ana" means inhale

- "Pana" means exhale

- "Sati" means mindfulness

Commonly referred to as the "mindfulness of breathing", primarily, it uses the breath as the object of concentration.

By focusing on the breath, one becomes aware of the mind's tendency to jump from one thing to the other.

The concept of breathing meditation is to bring your awareness and connection to your breath and breathing.

There are many different techniques for breathing meditations.

How do you do it?

An effortless way to begin a breathing meditation is to do square breathing.

- Count to four slowly while breathing in through your nose.

- Hold the breath for four seconds.

- Count to four as you release through your mouth.

- Hold for four seconds, then repeat from the beginning.

- Count slowly, feeling the sensation of the airflow on your nostrils. Tracing it all the way to your abdomen.

- Be aware of your stomach inflating as you take the air in and hold it. Feeling it deflate as you release the air and hold.

- Should you feel your mind wander, simply bring your attention back to the counting and the flow of your breath.

This meditation is an excellent and quick way to calm yourself down, and does so, by bringing your attention and focus into the present moment.

In a stressed, anxious, angry and worried emotional states, we tend to shallow breathe, further enhancing and prolonging the undesired emotion.

Focusing on your breathing, not only creates awareness of your breathing patterns (allowing you to adjust as required), the process creates a mind, body and breath connection.

As a simple practice with quick results, breathing mediation is an excellent practice for those looking to looking to manage unhelpful feelings and emotions.

Transcendental Meditation - TM

Developed by Maharishi Mahesh Yogi in the 1950's. Both the Marahrishi and the TM movement was popularised by The Beatles, The Beach Boys and other celebrities in the 1960's and 1970's.

Transcendental Meditation is attributed to bringing awareness of the practice of meditation to the mainstream in the West.

What is it?

TM is a type of mantra meditation, where the meditator focuses on a specific mantra for 20 minutes twice a day, seated and with closed eyes. TM allows the mind to settle and for the meditator to experience a peaceful and calm level of awareness.

How does it work?

To be able to practice TM, a practitioner must be initiated by a teacher.

Formal lessons and instruction are undertaken, followed by a ceremony whereby the teacher will provide the student with a personalised mantra.

The teacher will observe the student at three subsequent "checking sessions", with the student continuing to meditate for 20 minutes twice a day, indefinitely.

There are further levels of training available.

Walking Meditation

"If you are facing in the right direction, all you need to do is keep walking."

Buddhist proverb

In its official practice, walking meditation has specific spiritual and formal guidelines. However, the meditative and physical benefits can be achieved from a not so formally structured walk, and this is the philosophy behind the Happiness Hunter walks.

There are six guiding principles to The Happiness Hunter;

- Movement

- Stillness

- Awareness

- Focus

- Action

- Reflection

All of these can be achieved through the process of a normal, daily walk. The only requirement being that you "unplug" from any form of music/headphones and simply be present in your walk and environment.

For those who want to undertake a more formal process, there is the spiritual discipline of a walking meditation.

The Buddhist Zen practice of Kinhin is one example of this, where participants walk in single file accompanied by a clapper or bell.

The focus of meditative walking is to synchronise the breath and stride, with the purpose of developing present moment awareness, to become aware of yourself in your physical body.

What is it?

Walking meditation is like meditation in motion or action. Unlike a seated meditation with closed eyes and an inward focus, walking meditation is practiced with open eyes and awareness of surroundings.

A practice designed to help you become aware of yourself in your body, to fully engage your senses and to become more aware of yourself in the present moment.

How does it work?

Walking meditations has best results when practised outdoors, and in a place without traffic. Walking meditation is done slowly at a relaxed pace, it is not about covering vast distances.

Ideally, set aside 20 minutes for this meditation.

Find an open space. Stand still and become aware the soles of your feet on the ground and the subtle shifts that you are continually making to keep yourself balanced.

When ready, start walking in your usual manner. Noticing where your heel hits the ground and how the rest of the foot follows.

Become aware of your physical environment.

You can feel your attention drawn to the shape of a cloud in the sky, or the way the sunlight catches the leaves of a tree.

Perhaps, you could bring your attention to a bee buzzing around a flower, really focusing on how the petals of flower all work in harmony together, and how the colours change from the beginning of the petal to its end.

Feel your feet in your socks, and expand this awareness to your shoes.

Focus on relaxing your feet.

Focus on your ankles. Feel the way your ankles move to support your feet in motion.

Continue feeling into your body, feeling into each of the joints, ligaments, muscles, bringing your awareness to what is happening in your body as you walk.

Focus on a specific part of your body – what happens if you tense and release the calf muscle?

Now feel the sun or the wind on your body.

Notice where you feel the breeze or sun? Follow this body scan and awareness all the way up your body, into your hips, your pelvis, belly, back, shoulders and neck.

Feel the release of tension from your jaw.

Like all other types of meditation, as you become aware of thoughts and feelings or outside distractions, focus on observing them without attaching to them.

Keep bringing yourself back to the contemplative practice of your walking meditation.

To conclude your walking meditation, stop and stand still for a moment or two and experience yourself simply standing.

No longer in motion.

Ground yourself fully, by feeling the soles of your feet connected to the earth.

You can find out more about
The Happiness Hunter walks at
www.thehappinesshunter.com/walks

Binaural Beats Meditation

Although it is only through technological advancement of the past 100 years or so that binaural beats music as we know it has been created, sound repetition to entrain the brain has been around for many thousands of years.

Ancient cultures used consistent, rhythmic sound for many healing and spiritual benefits long before modern science proved the benefits of the process and long before it was called binaural beats.

How does it work?

Binaural beats meditation is a type of brain entrainment, using two tones of different frequencies to cause a physiological response inside the brain.

Binaural means; having or relating to two ears.

Therefore, to be effective, this practice requires earphones/headphones, as two different frequencies are sent and heard simultaneously through the left and right ears.

The mind perceives a third tone, which it calculates as the difference between the two frequencies. Causing the brain to follow the new third frequency, producing brain waves at that same level of Hertz.

You can listen to binaural beats to entrain your brain into different levels of consciousness.

How do you do it?

You can easily find a variety of binaural beats meditations via YouTube or a phone app.

It is a simple practice which can be undertaken by sitting or lying down as you would during a regular meditation.

Headphones are required to make this method effective.

While binaural beats are very safe, they are not recommended for those prone to seizures, and certainly should not be listened to while driving or using heavy machinery due to the deep relaxed state that they can induce.

Subliminial Affirmations Meditation

The first known usage of subliminal messages is with the Ancient Greeks, where they influenced people using a science called rhetoric.

In the mid-1800's, studies of how subliminal messages worked were undertaken for the first time, and in 1897 a book called The New Psychology by Dr. E.W. Scripture, was published which outlined some simple principles of how to use subliminal messaging for subtle persuasion.

How does it work?

Our mind works on three levels, the conscious (the part of our brain we use in an awake state), the subconscious (where our recent memories are stored) and the unconscious (where all memories and past experiences are stored. It is from our stored perceptions and memories and experiences that we form our beliefs, habits and behaviours).

The three minds work together, however, it is the conscious mind that directs the program, based on external or internal stimulus and it is the sub-conscious mind that retrieves the data, based on instructions from the conscious mind.

It is said that the human mind is 10% conscious, 50-60% subconscious and 30-40% unconscious.

What this means, is that 90% of our minds power comes from an old, dead energy – the past. Without taking control of our conscious mind in the present moment, and training our conscious mind to better utilize the information coming from our subconscious mind, or better yet, training the existing program to serve us up better information, we operate on auto pilot and continue with the same beliefs, habits and behaviours.

Unfortunately, the conscious level filter is created from personal belief systems and past experiences, which can be a real problem when the current belief system is not working for us.

The conscious minds job is to keep us safe.

Change (even when it is for our personal betterment and growth) can be seen as unsafe.

Therefore, to bypass these critical filters and limiting beliefs, we need to deliver the messages in a way which avoids our conscious awareness and filter. To do this, we need to use our conscious mind, in the present moment, to make the decision to change.

> ***The word 'subliminal' means below threshold, and this translates to any sensory input that is below the level of conscious awareness.***

Subliminal messaging is a powerful way to bypass critical thinking and logical reasoning to reach the subconscious mind directly.

In the context of a subliminal affirmations meditation, the meditation is designed to reprogram your subconscious mind, to then more positively influence your conscious awareness.

These meditations are an incredibly powerful way to create profound change, and are commonly embedded into a music track, where the conscious mind only hears the music.

By avoiding interference from our conscious thoughts, beliefs and/or experiences, the messages are accepted as a real and valid instruction by the subconscious mind.

Subliminal affirmations work through repetition, rewiring your brain and dissolving long-held belief systems and thought patterns (referred to as creating new neural pathways).

It is a powerful and extremely efficient way to create an abundance of positive thought processes, in turn helping you to change patterns of thinking and behaving (for example to be more confident, be more abundant, lose weight, sleep well).

Yoga

"The study of Asana is not about mastering posture. It is about using posture to understand and transform yourself."

unknown

With its rich history, Yoga dates back at least 5,000 years, with beginnings traced back to the Indus-Sarasvati civilisation in Northern India.

First mentioned in the Rig Veda (the oldest known sacred texts), containing collections of songs, mantras and rituals. There is evidence to suggest that it may be a tradition believed to be 10,000 years old.

What is it specifically?

Originally, a spiritual discipline, practised to harmonise and unite the body through body poses, breathing exercises and meditation.

The combination of mental, spiritual and physical practices (or disciplines), yoga has several pathways all leading towards the goal of experiencing truth, and the essence of our self.

Coming to the awareness of the West in the 20th Century, it is predominantly used here as a form of exercise and well-being.

How does it work?

Yoga is a simple step by step method that reverses the outward flow of energy and consciousness so that the mind becomes the centre of direct perception.

Because of its physical benefits to the body, yoga is not only used as a meditative means of uncovering thoughts, beliefs and emotions, it has now become a crucial element of any serious athletes training regime (including that of professional sports teams and athletes).

In additional to its spiritual purpose, from the physical perspective, yoga provides increased power, flexibility, and active-recovery process.

Through the mind and breath, yoga builds mental toughness.

Who is it for?

It may be easier to note who should not do yoga. With so many variations of this practice, ranging from the physically demanding to calm and relaxing it is a practice that anyone can undertake.

Benefits of a yoga meditation are almost immediate on every level; physical, emotional, mental and spiritual.

An excellent practice for those wanting to stretch, strengthen their body and mind at the same time.

In particular, Yoga can be perfect for those who struggle to stay focused on the present moment (as it is almost impossible to hold a challenging pose and not be completely present), and for anybody who would like to include an element of movement into their meditation.

** Seek out the guidance of an experienced teacher to safely teach you the correct postures.*

Writing

*"Start writing, no matter what.
The water does not flow until the faucet
is turned on."*

Louis L'Amour

Writing has the potential to be a powerful meditation practice.

When we write, we occupy a part of the brain that tends to get restless and looks for something to do, however, when we are writing, we are already doing something.

The practice of a writing meditation assists in integrating the active mind with the meditative mind, so if you are unable to sit still, writing is a great way to appease the active mind while practicing meditation.

It is similar to writing in a journal; however unlike journaling which has the objective of recording your day's activities and experience, a writing meditation is about observing your thoughts.

How do you do it?

You will need a notebook, pen, and a quiet space to sit comfortably. Begin by taking several deep breaths and become aware of the space you are in and how you are feeling. A great prompt to start your meditation practice is to write at the top of the page "right now".

Write for ten minutes without pause or editing. Simply write. Once finished, read aloud what has been written, being mindful of the thoughts, emotions and feelings that come up for you are you read it back.

Be mindful of judgment, criticism and expectations, in addition to the positive feelings.

Underline key words or phrases, make further notes if you like. The notes you make can be a prompt for future writing meditations, or you can simply use the words "right now" when you do your next one.

Incidental Moments & Repetitive Tasks

What is it?

There are many times in your day when you will already be meditating, even if it is by accident.

Accidental meditations happen when our left brain (which governs our language, rational thought, analysis and future planning), is occupied with a familiar and repetitive activity that does not require the full engagement of the brain.

Examples of this include driving a familiar route, where you 'suddenly' finding yourself at your destination, without any conscious recollection of how you got there.

Ironing and realising that you have pressed three shirts. Standing in the shower and not having any idea how long you have been there, or sitting in a waiting room staring at the wall.

How to do it?

Before you undertake a repetitive or familiar task, focus your attention on the activity at hand and become aware of yourself doing it.

We tend to consider many of the repetitive tasks that make up our daily lives as something that needs to be endured, as opposed to viewing them as an opportunity to be fully present in the moment. Brushing your teeth is one example. Walking to the car or store is a great opportunity to practice a mini walking meditation.

How To Develop
Your Meditation Practice

"Reality is for a man what he experiences
or knows at the present moment.

The experiences of yesterday are as unreal as dreams,
as long as he does not live them over again in thinking
and desiring. If he lives them over, they are in the present
moment, and become real again.

Thoughts of the future are only dreams,
unless these thoughts are felt and lived.

To the degree that they are felt and lived, they make
the present disappear, take its place and are reality."

Harold Waldwin Percival

While there are many benefits to doing active guided meditations (especially if that is what is working for you at the moment, by all means do not stop!).

There are other and further benefits to be experienced through a more passive meditation practice.

Any time you provide your mind to have a rest via a guided meditation is beneficial and never to be considered an inferior practice.

There are different benefits that you can start to experience as you become more comfortable with the practice of meditation and can learn how to just be with yourself and your thoughts with nothing else to direct the focus of your mind.

The reasons I first started meditating were primarily for mental and emotional health reasons (this perhaps may be the same reasons for you too).

However, my purpose quickly expanded into appreciating the physical benefits of meditation.

As my meditation evolved, my practice became a spiritual quest, and the more significant were my results.

So for you my friend, I want to share with you how you can introduce your passive meditation practice. Once you have had some practice with the guided meditations and feel ready to take things to the next level.

Remember; meditation is a practice and the only way you are going to get better is to practice.

How long you choose to meditate is up to you.

When first starting out, to give yourself the best chance of success, set yourself a timer.

I prefer to meditate for 30 minutes, and love it when I can practice for an hour or more at a time. However, some days, ten minutes may be all the time I have, or I may be interrupted by my children. This is perfectly ok.

A big part of your practice is letting go and accepting what is. Dr. Issam suggests that 24 minutes is ideal. This being one minute for every hour of the day.

But honestly, any minute of meditation is better than no time. Be ok with what you can do (without making excuses).

Using our senses helps us become aware of ourselves and our surroundings in the present moment. It also helps create the right environment for a meditation practice.

Our senses include; sight, hearing, smell, taste and touch/ feeling. Hence why we may light a candle, put on music, light incense, or use mala beads for our meditation.

All of which help to prepare us and create the space for us to get into a meditative state before we begin.

There are four channels of brain rhythm activity. At Beta A & B levels, our mind is very active, and where the majority of us (somewhere around 90%), spend most of our time.

We tend to get stuck in it.

On this level, we struggle to control our thoughts and emotions, which is why it can feel overwhelming and impossible to believe that we can meditate.

Using our senses, via music, candles, incense or visualisation to calm ourselves down and prepare ourselves for meditation, means that we can create the space to slow our brain rhythm.

As our brain rhythm slows, we can use visualisations to create further calm. For example, visualising yourself on a relaxing tropical beach or in an open green field.

From this space, we begin to operate on Alpha level, or the superconscious level, where we can be creative and use our imagination.

It is on this level that we meditate.

It is not difficult to switch between Beta, and Alpha levels and it can be done at any time. Meditation helps us to learn how to do this.

Our brain rhythms operate at the Theta or subconscious level and Delta or unconscious level during sleep.

How to Meditate

Step 1

Choose a time to meditate. Ideally, meditate at the same time each day in order to train your mind that it's time to have a break now. This means that when you do sit down for your meditation, your mind is already starting to prepare for what is going to happen.

The recommended time to meditate is sunrise and sunset (with that being said, any time is better than no time). Pick a time which best works for you.

Over the years, I've discovered the best time for me is to meditate is as soon as I wake up each morning. As a morning person, I enjoy waking early, it really is the best time of the day and it gives me the space and time to set my day up for success. Because I enjoy it so much and because I really feel the benefits from it, on most days, I also enjoy a subsequent meditation later on in the day as well.

I get up because I want to get up, say thank you for the day, set the intention that today is going to be a great day and make myself a warm lemon water. Sometimes I may light a candle (or not).

I will sit there quietly for a few minutes really focusing on being present and asking how I can best show up in the day, before I close my eyes and allow myself to drop into the stillness within.

Step 2

Wear comfortable clothes. It is important that your clothes are not tight or restrictive, as you want to feel loose and relaxed. Your clothing needs to support this feeling.

Step 3

Prepare your space. Light a candle, or some incense or you can put some music on. This will help you become aware of yourself, your surroundings in the present moment.

This will help to slow your mind down in preparation for your meditation.

Step 4

Choose a comfortable position.

Ideally, you want to be sitting with your spine straight, with your feet flat on the floor or with crossed legs, and with your hands resting loosely in your lap.

Alternatively, you may want to be lying down (with a straight spine), with your arms by your side.

This allows the energy to flow freely.

To enhance your practice, your focus and your posture and to increase the flow of energy, you can also try putting your fingers and hands into different positions – these are called "mudras". You can lightly touch your thumb with any of your other fingers (each position has a different purpose) or place your hands into the prayer position in front of your heart.

Step 5

If you are doing a guided meditation, close your eyes, and you can start listening now. If you are doing your passive meditation, take three deep breaths and focus on letting go.

Step 6

Close your eyes and feel yourself sink down into your heart space. It is helpful to focus on your breathing for a while, breathe in deeply, hold your breath, let the breath go and hold your breath.

Repeat.

Feel your breathing, be aware of your heart beating. Allow yourself to sink into this present moment. The only thing you are here to do right now is to let go. Let go of yesterday, last night, this morning. Let go of what you need to do later. You can think about that later.

Right now is all that matters.

Keep bringing your focus back to this moment now, into the breath, into your heart beat.

Step 7

Allow your thoughts to be.

Dr. Issam has a wonderful technique to learn to be the observer or be the watcher of your thoughts, while not engaging with them.

Imagine that you are in a car, stuck in mid-city traffic.

Imagine that the car you are in is a thought.

Now, feel yourself being lifted out of the car to the roof of the tallest building in the middle of the city. You can see for miles around you. You look down and see the cars and the traffic and the people below.

From this vantage point, the city looks beautiful, and everything has a place and a purpose, everything is flowing. But where you are, so high up, so far removed from the activity below, it's like you are entirely distanced from it.

It's nothing to do with you, and where you are now. You can observe it without any attachment, without any of it having any effect on you.

This is what is meant by being the watcher or the observer of your thoughts. You can watch them come and you can watch them go, but you don't need to go into them.

Step 8

Be mindful of how you are feeling. Are you holding tension anywhere?

Bring your breath into that place and feel the tension easing away.

Become aware of any thoughts and emotions that are arising.

Allow yourself to let them be and bring yourself back to your breathing.

Step 9

Go into the void. Between every thought, there is a space, a gap, a void, a nothingness.

Focus on the gap, focus on the void, focus on the nothingness.

Your passive meditation practice is about allowing yourself to let go of the thoughts to understand that there is this space, this gap… this void… this nothingness.

The goal is to allow yourself to sink into that space, into the gap, into that void, into that nothingness, the space that exists between your thoughts.

This is to experience yourself without thinking.

Step 10

Stay here in the stillness and the peace for as long as you like.

Keep bringing yourself back as you catch yourself going with your thoughts.

Allow them to be... keep letting them go.

Final Step

Complete your meditation.

*"Meditation is like going to the bottom
of the ocean, where everything
is calm and tranquil.*

*On the surface of the ocean there may be
a multitude of waves but the ocean is not
affected below. In its deepest depths, the
ocean is all silence. Fear, doubt, worry
and all the earthly turmoil's just wash
away, because inside us is solid peace.*

*Thoughts cannot touch us, because our
mind is all peace, all silence, all oneness.*

*When we are in our highest meditation,
we feel that we are the ocean. We feel that
we are the sky, and all the birds flying
past cannot affect us.*

*Our mind is the sky and our heart is the
infinite ocean. This is meditation."*

Sri Chinmoy

Guided Meditation Scripts

How to Use The Scripts

OPTION ONE:

You can read these scripts as part of your mindfulness/present moment practice.

Find a peaceful and quiet space where you will not be interrupted.

Sit, and focus your attention on the words of the script.

Read every word of the meditation out loud.

Pause frequently at the end of a line.

Breathe deeply on every full stop.

When you become aware of yourself drifting off into your thoughts, let the thoughts drift away and bring yourself back to the present moment.

Bring yourself back to the full stop and just focus there.

Take your time with the whole process to allow yourself to feel each word.

OPTION TWO:

Another great method is to record the scripts as you read them out loud. The majority of smartphones have quality voice memo apps pre-loaded; otherwise it is easy enough to find a free recording app.

Ensure you are in a calm and relaxed state prior to, and during recording.

Find a quiet space where you won't be interrupted. Speak slowly and clearly while pausing frequently.

There is power in the pause.

Allow for this space between words and sentences.

It is in this space, where you can start to practice going into the 'nothingness' that exists between your thoughts.

There is great power in using your voice to direct the focus of your mind.

OPTION THREE:

You can also read these scripts to guide your friends and loved ones through meditation.

Using a quiet, calm voice, speak slowly and clearly. Allow for space between the words, with long pauses between sentences.

There is no rush in meditation. It is a space to slow down and to go into the stillness and space within.

The scripts in this book are available as a recorded audio files via the following link;

www.thehappinesshunter.com/guided-meditations

Inner Sanctuary (Dr. Issam)

THIS MEDITATION WILL take you to your inner sanctuary.

As with each of these guides, be ok with whatever comes to you and don't over think, or try to analyse... just let it be and be present to whatever images, thoughts and feelings that come to you.

One of the first things you should do every time you need to feel calm, you need to feel relaxed, you need to empower yourself is to create your inner sanctuary.

Which exists within yourself, and you can go to that place any time you feel like energising yourself or balancing yourself.

Your sanctuary is your ideal place of relaxation... tranquility and safety... and you can create exactly as you wanted.

And now I would like you to imagine yourself
in some beautiful natural environment.

It can be any place that appeals to you.
In the meadow, on the mountaintop...
In the forest.

Beside the sea... it could even be under the
ocean. Or on another planet, wherever it is you
feel comfortable pleasant and peaceful to you.

You need to explore your environment.
Noticing the visual details...
The sound, smells, or any particular feeling
or impression you get about it to make it real.

Go for a walk when you're in your sanctuary
or for a swim. You can even fly...
Wherever you want.

You can build your own home, your own tent...
make it real as you are.

And now I want you to do anything you like to
do to make this place more at home like...
and comfortable an environment for you.

You might want to build some type of a house,
or shelter here... or perhaps just surround
the whole area with golden light of protection
and safety of healing... for your convenience
and enjoyment.

Or do as you will to establish it as your special
place, because it is your special place.

And from now on this is your own personal inner sanctuary to which you can return at any time... just by closing your eyes and desiring to be there.

And you will always find it healing and relaxing to be there.

It is also a place of special power for you.
You may wish to go there every time you do your creative visualization or for when you are trying to create a goal...and you might find that your sanctuary changes from time to time... or that you want to make changes and additions.

You can be very creative and have a lot of fun there and you can invite even special people to go there.

And when you are ready, I want you to take a deep breath...

And open your eyes... slowly... and shake your hands, shake your body... make sure that you did not leave half of you there.

Meeting Your Guide
(Dr. Issam)

THIS MEDITATION BY Dr. Issam, will help you connect with your meditation guide. Be open to whatever happens for you.

Connecting with your spirit guide can be a deeply moving and affirming experience. The voice, individual or feeling that you sense can give you strength and advice.

Finding your spiritual guide is a very personal process, and each individual will experience things differently. Some might even have to patiently wait for a long time before connecting with a spirit guide. Whenever you are meditating, you are still always in control.

Take a long deep breath, release that breath and feel yourself relaxing…

Welcome to this guided meditation and again,
find yourself a quiet place… to sit and calm,

Make sure that you are nice and comfortable...
Let your hands rest loosely in your lap.
And now close your eyes and just relax.

With your eyes closed, you begin to connect
with your inner world,
Inner world of thoughts... and feelings.
And give yourself permission
to enjoy this relaxation
Don't worry about anything... just let go.

You are free from any responsibilities for the
next 10 minutes, Put aside your thoughts or any
tasks you need to do later.... and remember, you
are always in control... and you can wake up
from this meditation anytime you want to.

Now take a long breath... and release that
breath… and feel yourself relaxing...
And one more time... take a long, slow deep
breath... And when you are ready,
let that breath go...
Take another one.... and when you are ready,
exhale, completely.

And feel the calmness creeping up your body
Continue to breathe, slowly, deeply... and gently

With each breath you take, your thoughts become quieter… And you feel the calmness
within you...

Allow yourself to relax now
Allow the gentle movement of your breath to
guide you... into a more relaxed state

Breathing in...
and when you are ready...
breathing out, and deeper you go.

Allow your mind to gradually slow down,
all by it self. And in your own time,
I would like you to create your inner sanctuary...
or go to your inner sanctuary, if you have already
got one...

Let go of any expectations, and allow yourself to
experience this journey,
Which will come to you naturally

Now see yourself anyway you like to be
It could be a grass field
It could be swimming
Feel the nature around you
Feel the warmth of the sun on your face...
and on your body

You can hear the sound of nature around you
You are very much at home, in this peaceful
place And you have all the time in the world
You feel safe...
And you feel happy

And take a moment to appreciate
everything around you
Using your five senses as well

And you notice, on your left hand side...
there is a big tree full with fruit...
And a small baby tree next to it.

I want you to walk towards those trees...
the closer you get, the more you notice
a little cave
A little bit beyond it....
I want you to keep walking towards that cave
You pass by the trees now... you are getting
closer and closer to the cave

And you start to notice that there is an old man
sitting there waiting for you...
Long white hair... and a long white beard.
I want you to greet him... tell him your name
And also ask him his name...
And take whatever name comes to you first.

And you also notice the man has a box for you...
a little gift

I want you to reach forward and take that box
from him and open it...
Because there is a message for you...
Open the box now and have a look at
what is inside... Try to understand this message...
and what it means for you

And now, thank the old man, and promise him
that you will meet him again

And now you need to keep walking back...
until you pass the trees
And this is your inner place that you can go to,
anytime you want to

Anytime you want to heal your body
Anytime you want to meditate

Now slowly and gently, open your eyes...
And still feel the calmness within you...
And focus on your breathing...
keep your eyes closed, focusing
on your breathing

And now, slowly and gently, open your eyes

Stand up... and shaking your physical body to
bring your energy back.

And that is good.

Meditation for The Breath
(Dr. Issam)

THIS MEDITATION IS designed to help you focus completely on your breath.

Welcome to this guided meditation.

In this meditation we'll teach you how to feel relaxed, and calm and become aware of your breathing.

Please find yourself a quiet place... and sit down, and just relax.

And make sure that you are nice and comfortable.

Let's begin... breathe in through your nostrils and breathe out when you're ready... and now breathe in again count to six.

One... two... three...four...five...and six

And now hold your breath counting to three
one... two ... three.

that's good... now breath out.

counting to three... One... two... and three.
Good. Now breathe in counting to six.

And now hold counting to three... that's good.

Now breathe normally... from your nostrils
and breathing out from your mouth.

And while you are breathing slowly...
I'll direct your breathing awareness... to different
stages of the breath.

...and focus all attention on my voice
and on your breathing.

One... notice the breath as it enters your nose.

Notice each time you breathe in...
and the way that breath feels on your nostrils...
feel the breath as it passes through...
and down along your throat.

How does it really feel?... warm or cold.

Just focus on the sensation... focus just
on the feeling of your breathing.

And also try to feel the breath going down to
your lungs and down your stomach...

And breathing out nicely and gently...
and every time you breathe just feel the air
expand your lungs... with each breath.

Feel the lungs expand and relax...
feel calm, feel relaxed.

And now turn your attention to the breath
travelling up and out through your mouth...
feel the breath in your throat... your mouth...
and across your lips.

Notice each breath as a whole now... and see
how the breath flows like waves... first in... you
pause... then out... then you pause... then out...

Then pause...

You now you feel calm and relaxed... relax.

Don't worry about your thoughts, let them
run... don't focus on them, let them be...
and just focus on yourself, how calm you feel
how relaxed you feel.

Pay attention to every muscle in your physical
body... Tense your muscles, and let it go.

Just to feel the difference between being tense
or being relaxed.

And tense your muscle again... and let go.

And if your mind keeps on wandering...
simply bring your awareness back to my voice
and to your breathing.

and keep focusing on your breath...
In and out.

This breathing is the breath of life...
What keeps you going.

Keeping you alive.

Breathe in and breathe out.

So focus on your breathing and relax.

Keeping your focus on your breath...
Don't lose your focus. Just your breathing.
Nothing else exists.

And now nicely and gently,
I want you to take a deep breath...
and when you are ready... breathe out.

That's good.

Meditation for Inner Peace & Harmony (Dr. Issam)

DR. ISSAMS' MEDITATION will guide you into a place of deep inner peace and harmony.

This meditation is to teach you how to return
to a state of inner peace and harmony... |
and reconnect with your inner world
or with your inner power.

And in a moment... when I say the word begin,
I want you to repeat silently in your mind every
single word I say.

Do not let your thoughts take your attention
away, not even for a single moment.

Just concentrate and relax.

Now... close your eyes and keep your eyes closed.

Begin... I'm going to relax myself.
I'm going to count from five to zero.

On or before the count of zero,
I shall be completely totally relaxed...

In mind. and in body.

Five...I can feel the muscles in my head....
my face... my jaw... relaxing.

Letting go completely.

More and more... further and further... relaxing.

Four... the muscles in my neck, my upper back,
my chest are letting go.
I can feel my muscles relaxing...
I can feel them letting go completely more.

And more relaxed.

Three...I can feel the muscles in my upper arms,
my forearms my hands, letting go...
I can feel that tension draining away from my
fingers... Draining away.

Fading away... further and further away...
as I relax completely.

Two… The muscles in my lower back...
My abdomen are letting go.
I can feel my muscles relaxing.

I can feel the tension drifting away further
and further. My muscles are becoming loose
and limp. Numb and dull... in fact my arms
have numb and dull feeling.

So very very relaxed.

My breathing is becoming deeper and deeper...
more and more regular... I am relaxing further
and further.

One... the muscles in my thighs and my lower
legs are relaxing.

I can feel the tension drifting away... more and
more every second. I can feel the muscles in my
feet letting go... so loose, and so limp...
so numb.

The tension is fading away.
I can sense that tension fading away...
More and more, every second.
I am becoming, so very, very relaxed.

So very, very relaxed.
Focus on your breathing...
And relaxing yourself more and more.

Not a care, not a worry, no fears, no anxieties.
Nothing will bother you or distract you.

Just relaxing now.

Letting go more and more.
In body and in mind.

You are now completely relaxed
completely calm.

Now just take a deep breath. slowly and gently
breathing in... and in... and out.
And now gently breathing out.

Now slowly open your eyes.
Shake your hands, shake your head, shake your
body... to make sure you are all working perfectly.

It's good.

Relaxing Your Mind, Relaxing Your Body (Dr. Issam)

THIS MEDITATION BY Dr. Issam, is about relaxing your mind relaxing your body and letting your imagination go wild to bring you to a place which will help to calm you down. The first step as usual is you need to focus on your breathing.

Breathe in slowly and deeply.
Take a few deep breaths, inhaling through your
nose and exhaling from your mouth.
Do not force your breathing,
stay calm and stay relaxed.
And let your breathing come naturally.

Each time you breathe in and you allow the air
to go to your lungs, you go deeper and deeper.

…and be aware of your breathing, be aware of
how deeply you breathe and you will being to
start to feel calmer and more relaxed.

Keep focusing your attention on your breathing.
Be aware of each breath you take through
your nose.

... and be mindful of each breath that you exhale
with your mouth.

Continue focusing on your breath.
And if you'll find your attention straying away
from the breath, just gently bring it back.

It will happen from time to time.
Do not be dis-heartened about it or upset, it's ok.

And what's important is to realise that when you
have wandered, then you move your attention
back to where it should be.

And the more you develop a greater focus the
easier it becomes to concentrate.

And now I need you to imagine that you are on
the shore of a beach and from afar you can see a
circle of people and guides sitting around a large
fire that has burned for eternity.

They see you walking toward them.
And they welcome you into the circle,
and they give you a seat to sit next to them.

And this is a chance for you to talk to these
people and to talk as well to your guides and
loved ones.

Or to anybody who you would like to talk to
The people gathered are all here because they
love you and want you to talk.
They want you to express.
They want you to tell them what is in your
heart. You can discuss with them everything
you like.

Or you can just sit back and listen as they tell
stories, and laugh and sing.

You are in this circle of friendship and laughter.
You can be absolutely yourself in here.
They all came for you, and they know your
heart. You know you are welcome and cherished.
And there is nothing you cannot do here.

You want to sing, you want to dance, you want
to laugh, you want to jump, you want to create.
You can do anything your heart desires.

To just be free.
Let your creativity be expressed in every shape
and form. Stay here for as long as you like.

And now I would like you to stand up in this
circle and hug everybody and tell them you
need to go and that you'll be back soon to see
them again.

And when you are ready. I would like you to
open your eyes and take a deep breath.

For a Great Night's Sleep

THIS MEDITATION IS to help you let of the day and to relax and calm your mental and physical body for a deep, relaxing and healing night's sleep.

Become aware of yourself lying on your bed.
Feel your head on the pillow.
Feel the softness of the pillow under your head.
Feel your head resting gently on the pillow.
Feel your body resting on the mattress under-
neath you. Become aware of your whole body
laying on the bed.

Feel the blankets covering your body. Take a
moment now to just shift your body around to
get into a comfortable position.

Take in a big deep breath through your nose and
hold it for three seconds before letting it all go.
Take in another deep breath, hold it for three
seconds before letting it all go.

… And take in one final deep breath, holding it for three seconds before letting it go.

… And if they aren't already, close your eyes, just feel your eyelids gently closing over your eyes.

Let the day be.

Now is the time for you to allow yourself to sleep, to let your mind let go, to feel your body relax, to let go of the events of the day and to allow yourself to drift gently off into a deep and relaxing sleep.

You will awaken in the morning deeply re-freshed, positive and ready to move through the day with ease and grace.

Now is the time to simply focus now on your breath. Every time you feel your attention mov-ing away from your breath, bring yourself back to the breath.

Bring yourself back to your body lying on the bed, letting the day close quietly around you. What's done is done, what's not done, is not done. The day is over, the time for sleeping is here now.

This is your time to simply allow yourself to sleep, to allow yourself to let go and to focus on your breath and your deep, slow breathing.

In an out, in and out.
Bring all your attention to your breathing.

Become aware of the flow of breath through
your nose, and visualise the oxygen flowing into
your lungs, into your heart.

See the oxygen flowing through your blood
stream and into all of the organs of your body.

Feel the oxygen moving through all of the
cells of your body, filling them up with fresh,
clean air.

Let the breath move through your body, in and
out, in and out, in and out.

When the thoughts come to your head,
when images of the day try and show themselves
to you asking for your attention, accept that
they are there, that they will come but that they
can go.

They can all wait until tomorrow.
Right now, the time is simply here to focus
on your breath, to allow yourself to let go,
to allow yourself to have a deep and refreshing
nights' sleep.

The events of today will still be there tomorrow.
You can deal with them then if you need to.

Now is the time for sleep, now is the time for
letting go, now is the time to just focus
on your breath.

Bring your attention back to your breath, feel
the air flow in through your nose, feel yourself
becoming more and more deeply relaxed.

Feel your body releasing all of the day's tension.
Feel your muscles let go.
Breathing in and breathing out.
Breathing in and breathing out…

Breathing in and breathing out…
Breathing in and breathing out…
Breathing in and breathing out…

When the thoughts come in,
you can let them go.
Let them come, let them go.
Do not focus on them, do not go with them.

Just see them and watch them drift away.
Focus all your attention now on your breathing.
Breathe in, breathe out.

Feel your whole body becoming more
and more deeply relaxed.
Feel your mind slow down.
Let the day go, let the day be, let the day rest.
Now is the time for deep, healing,
replenishing sleep.

Now is the time to let your body rest.
Now is the time to let your mind rest.
Simply let go of the day.

Let the day go.
Let the thoughts go.

Focus on your breath…
Breathing in…
Breathing out…
Feel your breath becoming deeper and deeper…
Slower and slower.
Feel yourself just letting go as you drift off into a
deep and relaxing sleep.
Focusing on your breath, in and out in and out.

You will have a deep relaxing
nights sleep tonight.
You are having the best nights sleep you have
ever had in your life.
You will awaken in the morning feeling positive
and refreshed and able to respond to the events
of the day.

Breathing in and breathing out.
Feeling your whole body now is deeply
deeply relaxed. Just let your body feel the breath.

Let the breath heal your mind and your body.
Let the deep air flow.
In and out in and out.

The Future You Meditation

THIS POWERFUL GUIDED visualisation meditation is to help you get clear on who you would like to be in your life and what you desire for the experience of your life.

Take a moment to centre yourself.

Take in a big deep cleansing breath, feel it enter your nose and move gently all the way down to the bottom of your diaphragm.

Hold it there for a moment, before releasing.

Now take in another deep cleansing breath and feel it cleanse all of the old stale air, refreshing your lungs and travelling all the way into your blood stream, through your body and into your heart.

Feel your heart beating.
Feel your heart expanding as the breath enhances the feeling of peace and harmony within your body.

Keep breathing deeply as you feel this life giving oxygen travelling to every part of your body, revitalising you cells, and creating a peaceful and harmonious sense of balance within your physical body.

Now, I would like you to clear your mind of all of its thoughts…

Visualise the breath that is coming into your lungs moving its way through your body and into your head.

Feel all the thoughts and worries and cares and concerns being gently sent off by this breath out into the Universe.

Feel the peace descend over your mind as you allow it to become clear of all of your worries.

In this space of open ness and freedom I want you to see your mind as a blank canvas.

You are the artist… You are the creator…

You can design whatever you want to see, feel and experience in this blank beautifully clear space… In this space, all of your desires can be fulfilled.

There is nothing that cannot be achieved here. Anything you want to create, you can create. Anything you want to see, you can see.

Anything you want to experience,
you can experience. Anything you want to hear,
you can hear.

You can be joined in this space by anyone you
like. There are no rules here… and there are
no limits.

Your potential is infinite and endless.
Keep breathing deeply.

With every breath you take, your mind
is becoming clearer and clearer.

There is so much light around you.

It's like a brilliant white gold light.

You can feel this light spreading all through your
body, showering down upon you.

This beautiful bright light enters your head and
clears out any remaining worries and cares and
concerns.

They are gone.

There is no room for them here with this beautiful healing light.

Your mind is clear.

You are free here and now to visualise your
amazing self, to get to know the future you.

There is so much power in being clear on where you want to be in your life, on who you want to be, how you want to be living it and what you want the experience of your life to be.

Bob Procter has said; if we can see it in our minds eye, we can hold it in our hands.

The clearer you can see the you that you want to be, the more intensely that you can feel it, the more deeply you are going to draw the opportunities, people, events and circumstances towards you so that you become this person.

The clearer you are, the better decisions you will begin to make, the better choices you will take. Firstly, I want you to look out at this blank canvas.
It is in front of you… it is above you… it is beside you… it is below you… it is behind you.

Feel yourself turning in a 360-degree circle, seeing nothing but a blank canvas around you.

You look down at your hands.
There is nothing to see.
It is like you are invisible.
It's like you too are a blank canvas.
Whatever may have existed before…
it is no more, everything is fresh…
it's like you have a brand new slate.

Anything you create from here is real,
all of your visualisation holds within it the seeds
of new beginnings.

Slowly, you start to see this blank canvas start to
take shape. Colours start to become clearer.
Shapes start to form.

It's becoming clearer where you are.

You start to see that where you are right now is
the ultimate place of peace and joy for you. It
may be a tropical beach, with the sun shining
brightly over miles and miles of white sand, with
clear turquoise water lapping at the shore.

It may be a beautiful rainforest with the sun
cascading onto the forest floor, with glorious
butterflies floating past you.

You may be on a secluded beach
or under a waterfall.
You could be somewhere you have
never been before, somewhere you have always
wanted to visit.

You can be anywhere and you can go anywhere.
Wherever you are, it is a very peaceful place to
be and you feel a great sense of joy knowing you
are exactly where you are meant to be.

You belong here.

For the next few breaths, I would like you to make this place as real as possible.

Add anything you want to have here, anything you want to see.

Now, I would like you to see yourself as you would like to be.

Remember, there are no rules here.
It is as though you are looking at yourself from the outside.

You can see the physical shape of your body, the strength within your body, the colour of your hair, the length of your hair.

See yourself really starting to take shape and see yourself exactly as you would like to be. You look at your face and see the most beautiful smile you have ever seen.

You feel such a sense of love and acceptance for this wonderful person.

For the first time in your life, you are seeing yourself through the eyes of absolute love and absolute compassion.

This person is really you.
This confident, happy, smiling, person is you.

What does perfect health mean for you?
What activities are you doing to fill your day?
What does success mean for you?

What would make you feel so amazing to be
living in this body?

Next, I want you to really feel into the sensa-
tions of being in this place.

It is like you are now in that body, you are that
person that just a moment before you were looking at from the outside.

I want you to now look at the environment you
are in through your own eyes.

Look down at your hands. Turn them over.

Feel how comfortable you feel in this body; how
much you belong to be here.

Become aware of the wind gently caressing
your face. Feel the sun warming every part of
your body.

You have never felt such a sense of peace
to be you.

I want you to imagine what kind of feelings you
are experiencing in your life.

Feelings of contentedness, of love, of abundance, of possibility, of joy.

Think about all the things that make you the great person you are.

All the things that you are doing to create these feelings in your life on a daily basis.

I want you to now visualise the life that you are living. Is there anybody with you sharing your life with you?

I want you to visualise those people and those relationships.

Feel the love and acceptance you have for these people. Feel the love and acceptance that they have for you. Spend some time here feeling the connection.

Feel the support… Feel the sense of unity.
Now, I want you to get clear on what you are doing in your life.
Are you working? …
Are you retired?
Are you a great humanitarian?
Are you a hugely successful entrepreneur?
Are you a parent?

Remember, this is your very own blank canvas, you can create here whatever you like.
Are you an author? …

A speaker?
Do you care for animals?

What does a successful life or career
look like for you?

Feel how easy it is to be doing this work.
You are so good at it…
You were born to be doing this.
This is where you belong.

This is your passion. This is your gift.
This is your purpose.
This is what you were born to do.

What a great gift it is that you are so clear
on what it is you are meant to be doing
with this life.

You feel such a sense of peace and accomplish-
ment that you are living your life with such
meaning and purpose.

Let yourself say clearly in your mind.

I am happy and successful in all that I do.
I love my life and I feel so grateful every second
of every day that this is what I get to do
with my life.

Where are you living?
It's like where you are starts to fade away
and a new shape takes place.

You realise that it is your dream house.
And it is where you live.

You put your hand in your pocket and feel the
house keys. It is a comforting feeling.

Visualise yourself looking at your house from the
outside, it is like you are 20 metres away. What
does your house look like from this distance?

As you walk closer towards the house, more and
more detail starts to become clearer.

You can see the windows, and the colour you
have chosen. As you walk towards the front
door, you feel such a sense of peace and content-
ment that this is your home.

You belong here.

You reach again into your pocket for the front
door key and open the door.

Entering into this haven, you feel yourself relax.
You are home.

This is where you belong.

Now I want you to feel that this person is really
you. I want you to know that this person is you
right now. You are this person.

You are this person in this moment now.

There is no time or space. From now on,
every choice you make, every decision you take
is this you.

This you, the you that has been created from a
blank canvas.

This you is real.

This is the real you.

You can stay here as long as you like.
When you are ready, open your eyes.

Welcome home.

Confidence & Success

YOU CAN DO this meditation at any time, especially before a big meeting, conversation, or whenever in need a confidence boost.

This is called progressive muscle relaxation and you can do this at any time when you are feeling tense and anxious. You simply exaggerate the feeling of tension in your body, feel it deeply and hold it there, before focusing on releasing it and letting it go.

Sit or lie comfortably.

Take a big deep breath in and as you release it, close your eyes.

Feel all the tension draining away, feel all the tension leaving your body.

Let your breath find it's own deep, natural rhythm.

Now you are going to shift your focus to different parts of your body, to create as much tension as you can, before releasing it.

Exaggerate the movements as much as you can, to feel as deeply into each of the parts of your body as you can, being aware of how you are holding the tension and how it feels in your body.

Feel the relief in letting it go and feeling your body relax into its calm and natural state.

To start, scrunch your feet up as tightly as you can, feel your toes deeply curled under your feet. It's ok if you feel your face scrunching up at the same time. Hold this tension for the count of ten…

One… two… three… four… five… six… seven… eight… nine… ten …
and now release it.

Feel all of that tension drifting away through the soles of your feet, though your toes. You can gently move your feet and your toes and feel the difference.

Now, I want you to move up to your calves. Tense them as tightly as you can. Feel the tension in your ankles and knees as well. Hold that tension there again for the count of ten;

One… two… three… four… five… six…
seven… eight… nine… ten …
and now release it.

Moving up to your thighs and buttocks. Clench
your thighs and buttocks as tightly as you can.
And when you think you can't clench anymore,
I want you to see if you can clench even harder.
Hold it there for the count of ten.

One… two… three… four… five… six…
seven… eight… nine… ten … and now release.

Now become aware of your stomach
and lower back.

Focus on tightening your pelvic floor and
clenching your stomach muscles. Hold this
tension for ten seconds.

One… two… three… four… five… six…
seven… eight… nine… ten …
and now release it.

Your whole body is now starting to feel heavy
and deeply relaxed.

Ball your hands into fists and squeeze them as
tightly as you can.

Tense your lower arms and upper arms, and then
tense them a little bit more.

Hold this tension for ten seconds

One… two… three… four… five… six…
seven… eight… nine… ten … and now release.

Feel how heavy and relaxed your arms
and hands are.
Focus now on your shoulders.

This is where you carry the weight of the world.

Today, you are going to release all of that
pressure and tension and feel free of all
your cares and worries.

I want you to tighten and lift your neck muscles
as close to your ears as you possibly can.
Your shoulders are leaning right into your neck.

Create as much tension here as you possibly
can. Now hold it for ten seconds One… two…
three… four… five… six… seven… eight…
nine… ten …

… and now let you shoulders fall and feel the
deep relaxation of just letting it all go.

Now, I want you to move to your face.
Crunch you face up as tightly as you can.
Feel your brow tightening, close your eyes as
hard as you can and feel your jaw tense.
Feel the tension all over your scalp,
and hold it here for ten seconds,

One… two… three… four… five… six… seven… eight… nine… ten … and now release.

Your whole body is now heavy and completely relaxed.

If there is any tension anywhere in your body,
I want you to become aware of it and to breathe
deeply into that space.
Focus now on breathing in slowly and deeply
through your nose and releasing slowly
and gently through your mouth.

Now, I would like you to listen to the words
I am going to say to you.

I want you to follow my words only and focus
on what I am saying.

Keep breathing deeply and comfortably, but I
want you to focus on the words and be aware of
the pictures in your mind.

Allow yourself to feel the positive emotions of
what I am saying. I want you to know that every
word I say is the truth. Focus on being deeply
relaxed and repeat these words in your mind.

I feel calm… I feel relaxed… I feel confident.
I feel a great sense of ease.
My mind is clear.

I can do anything I set my mind to.
Success is a state of mind…
My state of mind is a successful state of mind.

I speak with confidence… I listen…
I respond with confidence.

I give myself time to respond.
I believe in myself.

I know my value… I am valuable…
I know my worth… I am worthy.

I deserve success

I am successful.
I succeed at anything I put my mind to.
I can feel successful right now.
I am successful right now.

I allow myself to feel calm and confident

I think calm and positive thoughts.

I am calm… I am relaxed… I am confident…
It all feels very easy.

I allow for it to be easy.

Stay here now in this space of feeling deeply
calm and relaxed.

You are calm, you are confident.

You are completely supported in all ways.

Know that you can do anything you set your mind to. Within you is a power and a force that is greater than your mind.

Allow this power and this force to help you feel calm, confident and successful.

Now I want you to slowly bring your awareness back to your breath and into your body.

You are an amazing and incredible human being and today you are going to do amazing things.

Now open your eyes and go take on the world.

A Note to a Friend

> *"There are no strangers here;*
> *only friends you haven't yet met."*
>
> William Butler Yeats

THANK YOU.

It is an incredible honour knowing you have taken the time to read this book.

I truly do hope it delivered everything you hoped it would and more. If you've got any questions, or want to share anything about what you have discovered, please email me;

Fiona@thehappinesshunter.com

I would love to hear from you.

The purpose of writing this book was to provide you with a simple and practical introduction into the life changing practice of meditation, together with methods and scripts for the beginner (all the things I myself craved and needed as the beginner in this journey).

Meditation changed my life for the better, and it continues to do so.

And this is my wish for you, too.

My mission and purpose in writing this book was to share the message and benefits of meditation, to simplify the practice and to debunk the stereotypes.

Yes, you can do it.

Yes, it will change your life.

Yes, it really is that simple.

And everybody (especially you) can do it!

I wanted to unpack everything I know, and have learned (including sharing some of the wisdom of my teacher and guide Dr. Issam) and give it all to you, in a way that made you feel like you really can do this.

Yet it is you, who has given to me (even before this book went to print and you turned the first page)… it is you who has given to me.

In the process of writing this book, I was forced to reflect on my own meditation practice.

You see in order to teach, I needed to go back, to revisit my younger self, at the beginning of this journey. To look also at my current practice and towards my future.

To remind me;

- That while I have overcome some old stories and belief systems, with each new level of growth, these unhelpful thoughts have an opportunity again to present themselves.

- That knowledge and awareness are nothing without understanding and action (the learning is in the doing).

- Meditation gives to and enhances my life in the most beautiful and unexpected of ways.

In the purpose and the act of wanting to give to you, my reader, to share with you all that I know of meditation, it is actually you who has given to me. And for that I am eternally grateful.

With thanks, and with all my love,

Fiona

Dr. Issam Kadamani

DR. ISSAM KADAMANI MSCD
M. IMM (Aust) M. NMI (Aust)
Alumni USA, Reiki & Sekhem
Master, Ajna™ Tibetan Healing
Grand Master.

With 35-years spent teaching around the world, Dr. Issam is based in Melbourne as the Principal at The International College of Meditation & Healing.

Dr. Issam's mission is to empower his students to life their lives in full, with unconditional love and joy.

He does this by running seminars and workshops, teaching meditation, metaphysics and providing much sought after life coaching, counselling, healing and spiritual mentoring for those looking to learn a happier way of living.

With a deep awareness of his destiny and life path from an early age, at age seven, Dr. Issam's grandfather, taught him about understanding the power of thought, listening to his inner voice and about showing compassion towards others.

With his grandfather's encouragement and guidance, Dr Issam began to meditate when he was 8. With his first vision (aged 13), he saw his homeland of Lebanon at war. Three months later, his vision became a reality, and his homeland became a dangerous place.

Captured by a rebel group and imprisoned, suffering from hunger, torture, solitary confinement and starvation.

After his release, Dr Issam and his grandfather were visited by an elderly man named George, who informed them of the young Dr. Issam's next stage of life; spending time at a Mystery School in Tibet, where he would learn to meditate deeply to reach a "bliss" state, to heal others through Ajna™ Tibetan Healing.

To see and read auras clearly and effortlessly as well as astral travel. With more than three years spent learning at this school, Dr. Issam then furthered his study, by spending time in the Great Pyramid of Cheops in Egypt, Le Chateau in France and with different Masters throughout Europe, prior to coming to Melbourne.

www.drissam.com
www.icmh.com.au

*"The gift of learning to meditate
is the greatest gift you can give yourself
in this lifetime."*

Sogyal Rinpoche

www.ingramcontent.com/pod-product-compliance
Lightning Source LLC
Chambersburg PA
CBHW051451050726
47593CB00005B/2026